A Course in Time Travel

By

Curtis Loys Jackson, DM

Birch and Aspen
Publishing

First Edition, 2014

ISBN: 978-0-9921627-6-4

Birch and Aspen Publishing
Ottawa, ON
Canada
www.birchandaspen.com

CONTENTS

Contents

Contents

Chapter 1

Open Eye Meditation

Open Eye Meditation is easy to learn, and by far, the most powerful meditation on the planet! Take a look at *Figure 1.1* showing the physical points to concentrate upon. The beauty of this meditation is that it occupies the mind by requiring it to concentrate upon two things at the same time. This allows the *Future You* or *Oversoul* to begin to manifest within your field of consciousness.

Do Not Disturb

Select a quiet, comfortable place to sit down where you will not be disturbed. Sit in a comfortable position and pick two objects to concentrate upon. Pick an object to the left of you to look at with your left eye and pick another object to the right of you to look at with your right eye.

It is important to stay aware of both objects and keep them in your peripheral vision. Concentrate upon the equal and continuing awareness of them. To do otherwise is to drop out of meditation. Once these are fixed, you can begin to be aware of the field of view in front of you, but not at the expense of losing focus on either object[1].

This is a progressive meditation which means that you will experience more, the more you do it. Some of our members in Europe have even begun using Open Eye Meditation instead of drugs to enhance their consciousness at rave dances.

Quiet Expectation

It is helpful to cultivate an attitude of quiet expectation. Be aware of a heightening of senses. Quiet any fears that might arise, nothing can hurt you. Be prepared for feelings of overwhelming happiness, but be patient if it does not come right away. You may become aware of sights and sounds that you have never experienced before. Relax and enjoy them. They were there before you became aware of them and they can not hurt you. In the beginning only meditate between five minutes minimum and twenty minutes maximum.

---

[1] Please *blink* your eyes *normally* during Meditation.

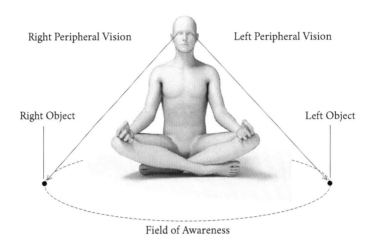

Figure 1.1: Open Eye Meditation

While you are meditating, it is important to stay in the meditative state. If your focus strays from the fundamentals described above you will not be in *Open Eye Meditation*. If we try too hard or are too serious this can be detrimental to experiencing the kinds of joy and Cosmic understanding that is available. If we are afraid or holding on too tight we will experience very little until we let go. Letting go and accepting is a forever process. The faster we do it the more fantastic it becomes.

A Course in Time Travel is designed to help people discover and bring into being innate but hidden potential that was not normally available in this time period.

Imported from the Future

The techniques and information found here are imported from the remote future by a group of Time Travelers called the *Collective*. Each of us has a time traveler from the future, called a *Time Traveling Oversoul* (TTO), that is part of this group. What this means for you is an unprecedented opportunity to increase your power and level of consciousness to any degree you desire.

Two Major Approaches

There are two major approaches you can use to reach this objective. The first approach is through a very special series of techniques, which are related to meditations, but much more powerful and advanced. Most meditations taught today take you to specific areas within your consciousness to experience various vibrations and lessons. The techniques included in this course allow an incomprehensibly advanced and wonderful part of you to become available to you as part of your natural evolutionary progression.

The Manifestation Takes Place in Stages

1. The introductory period that can last many life times. During this period, mutual trust builds between you and your TTO. Although you may not be fully aware of this on a conscious level, there is an exertion of irresistible influence upon you and your decisions.

2. A period of conscious awareness and communication with this part of you. During this period the Student actively strives to cause progressive levels of Cosmic Consciousness through intense study, meditation and group consciousness.

3. This period is the gradual metamorphic transition from Three-Dimensional *Human* Consciousness to Multidimensional *Super Human* Consciousness.

The Second approach provides you with an understanding of the nature of your Consciousness that was not available in this time period. The information comes from many thousands of years in the future and willprovide you with the most advanced knowledge and techniques available on the planet today.

If we desire change then we must be willing to allow change. It is helpful to remember that we are trading in the old self that is a faded remnant trapped thousands of years ago in the past, by merging with a new self that is more wonderful than we could ever have dreamed for.

CHAPTER 2

INTRODUCTION TO TIME TRAVEL

What if Time Travel is a Universal process of unfolding that is taking place all around us, without our knowledge? Wouldn't its presence be easily recognized by the necessarily profound metamorphic resultant changes in our neighbors? Or are we blind to these super-human visitors due to (protective?) limitations in our three-dimensional awareness? Are there human beings in our midst as advanced to us as we are to the ape?

First Hand Knowledge

If this is indeed true, (and I am stating from first hand knowledge, and many years as a time traveler, that it is), what can you do to be a part of this amazing phenomenon? What follows is not for the faint of heart, and cannot be mastered in a few minutes. It is a gradual and continuous balanced expansion of consciousness and understanding that guides you, step by step, from your very safe, (very busy?), everyday existence and transforms you into a *super* version of yourself. A state of being that has just been waiting for you to realize and acquire. A state of being that is most likely far beyond your wildest dreams.

It has long been held that just outside of our scope of understanding, we are all-knowing. If this is true, wouldn't it behoove us to seek knowledge and help from this omniscient part of ourselves in order to facilitate our efforts to Time Travel? Better yet, wouldn't it be amazing if this part of us that knows how to time travel could be here with us all of the time so we could learn this and other wonderful things from it? To this end, the material provided for you in this book, has given you a proven step by step procedure on how to open a "time portal" from within your own consciousness. This precious information has been painstakingly imported from the far future, and is not currently available anywhere else in the world.

Countless Lifetimes

The many years of 3D existence, so heavily ingrained in all of us, that normally prevent us from exposure to our inherent multidimensional reality, needs somehow to be left behind as new understanding takes its place. Rather than wallowing in the old ways and old problems, with antiquated solutions that rarely worked, we at Time Travelers stress merely leaving the old behind and incorporating the *new*, like shedding an old skin. This means rather than trying to accomplish something, we simply accept that it is already done. I know this sounds overly simplistic and easy, but once you have had success in doing it this way, it will seem miraculous. You will wonder why you have been working so hard spiritually *not* to achieve success, when success was already yours? It always was.

Let me hasten to add that persistent work in the form of study and practice of the techniques taught here in *A Course in Time Travel*, is vitally important and necessary if you are to succeed.

Re-Education

In our course we have included all of the necessary exercises, that have worked for us and are working for many people from all over the world. These exercises are designed to help reeducate the stubborn 3D mind and help pry lose its frantic grasp of prevailing earth bound concepts. If you do these exercises on a daily basis for a few minutes a day, your results can be phenomenal. We suggest making a set time each day for your studies and exercises. It is better to be consistent and to digest the material slowly, settling in for the long haul and your rewards will be spectacular.

When we normally speak of the Third Dimension we are talking about a collection of the First, Second and Third Dimensions. Each of these places is a composite part of what we consider our three-dimensional Universe. Each separate dimension has its own special set of rules and kind of time. Each has its counter part (polar opposite), in the fourth dimension. We need to learn a little about these component dimensions, so we can fully appreciate the Third and Fourth Dimensions as a single functioning dimension called the *Fifth Dimension*.

Two Major Sections

A Course in Time Travel is laid out in two major sections. The first section consists of greatly enhanced knowledge imported from the future. This knowledge explains, in easy to learn steps, the secrets of time travel and multidimensional consciousness. Discussed in detail are subjects such as the *Twelve Chakra System*, and the *Twelve bodies* that comprise your inner being[1].

The second section consists of all the techniques needed to access multidimensional consciousness and the ability to time travel. This is the *How-to* section. These techniques are thoughtfully laid out and explained in easy to understand layman terms.

Below is a partial list of subjects covered:

1. The *Illusion* of time.

2. Automatic self-maintenance of the past.

3. How the *illusion* of time is created by the Soul.

4. What are some of the problems for the Oversoul trying to communicate with the residual consciousness residing in the remote past.

5. "Time loop" a trap from which there is no natural escape.

6. What we can do to break free from the illusion of time.

7. The Soul's revelation in the remote future concerning "time" and its re-manifestation into the past.

8. Why our techniques for manifesting multidimensional consciousness here in the third dimension work, and why all other systems contained in this time period do not.

9. Why we could never have found the necessary tools for manifestation in our present time frame without help from our *Future Self*.

10. How to avoid all the multidimensional traps (this information alone is worth its weight in gold).

---

[1] Neither of these amazing revelations were previously known or taught in this time period.

CHAPTER 3

INTRODUCTION TO TIME TRAVEL

Be patient while reading through these Chapters. They are designed to subtly deprogram and enhance your sub-conscious 3D grasp of time/space reality. This process takes place whether your conscious mind understands all that it reads or not. Your subconscious/super-conscious mind, which does understand, will be eager to absorb this information.

Although we as Time Travelers usually travel in groups[1], we belong to no particular race or country. You cannot look at a person who has not yet returned from the future, and tell if they are a potential Traveler to this time period or not. There is simply no way of knowing. However, when they do return, they will begin to act differently. Travelers do not always come in at birth. They may walk in at any time, during the incarnation.

Travel into the past is absolutely necessary because it leads to certain essential realizations, that can eventually free one from the limitations of time and space, and facilitate the rediscovery of unimaginably wonderful states of being. This is a natural part of the phenomenon of human metamorphosis.

You are becoming a Time Traveler through the natural progression of your Soul, experiencing a vast array of possible futures, over many life times. At some point, an astounding realization is made by the Soul, that all futures are degenerative. That the primary lesson learned by experiencing the future is, that the act of it somehow violates a fundamental law of balance.

Although it was necessary for our Souls to experience the future, and to create a structure in time, the act of doing so, has taken them far from the actual natural center in time, and has caused them to experience all manner of unseemly realities.

It is at this moment of realization that your Soul gladly lets go of the illusion of future/past, and gravitates automatically, into nonlinear time, to begin the nurturing process for *all* of its past incarnations.

The Soul, by the act of transcending linear time, begins to achieved a state of spiritual equilibrium within the personalities trapped in each

---

[1] Souls tend to reincarnate in groups.

of its lifetimes. This point is not selected, but is reached as a natural result of letting go, by the Soul, of the concept of time altogether. This results in the Soul attempting to re-manifest into *all* of its past incarnations[2].

---

[2] This concept will be explained in more detail as we progress through the Chapters.

Chapter 4

The Third and Fourth Dimensions Compared

We can assume there is a basic difference between the *Third* and *Fourth* Dimensions, but exactly what are these differences and how do they affect us?

One way to look at this question is by thinking of the Fourth Dimension as being equal and opposite to the Third Dimension. A mirror image in the purest sense. Every equal aspect is inside-out, upside-down, and backwards from one another. This line of thinking would place the two dimensions in a perfect state of counter-balancing forces. The third and fourth dimensions are actually two opposite halves of one thing, the fifth dimension.

We can think of the third dimension as outward-facing or as having six directions of *out*[1]. This would mean, from the above definitions, that the Fourth Dimension, being *exactly* equal and opposite, would have to have six directions of *in* as its composition.

In the third dimension it seems as though we have access to the direction of in, but is this a fact in reality, or is it just an illusion? When examined more closely, the direction of in is really a direction of through, (as into an apple), which is actually just another direction of *out*.

We have established that our three-dimensional viewpoint is from a single point to all directions of out. To simulate a 4D viewpoint, we would have to establish a viewpoint coming from everywhere, converging upon a single point.

Intuitive Flash

As you might imagine, time travel cannot be achieved by intellectual means alone. It has been said, "To understand a thing is not the same as being able to do that thing". This especially applies here, for there is a fine line between accomplishment on these subtle planes of existence, and simply day dreaming. It is thought that our innermost self, on its own level, processes information in very general terms, or abstractions. This means you need to gather specific and detailed information

---

[1] Up, down, left, right, forwards and backwards.

through your physical mind, in order to process it and formulate new abstract concepts.

Sometimes we have what is called an *intuitive flash*, an instantaneous flood of understanding. It sometimes takes years to fully comprehend the massive amounts of new material that becomes available with even a single intuitive flash. The average person is lucky to have one event like this in an entire lifetime, and when it does occur, it changes that individual's viewpoint dramatically. A high-grade "genius" can learn to force intuitive flash through a process of force-feeding the mind with all aspects of a question until a flash occurs.

It is possible for a fully functioning Time Traveler to receive intuitive flashes directly from the Innermost Self as the most efficient form of communication. This would endow the traveler with astounding powers of perception, and an unbelievable amount of knowledge, much of which is new to this time period. Without preparation, this form of communication might wreak havoc upon the fragile and unsuspecting personality. With practice, the time will eventually come when the Time Traveler experiences and accepts a state of continuous intuitive flash as a normal state of being.

Perfection

It is believed by many that we, as human beings, have within us the guaranteed possibility of existing in a most fantastic way, as compared with what we consider *normal* existence.

Each subtly gradient *sub-reality*, in which we seem to exist, are merely fragments of a perfect *super-reality* just beyond our realization. If this is true, then remove even a single one of these sub-realities—no matter how insignificant—and the super-reality, by definition, would cease exist.

This concept would certainly justify some of the bizarre circumstances and experiences of life and living, as being necessary subcomponents created by each of our Souls, as part an immense group karma, spanning vast amounts of time.

Here is a simple example is this idea: if we observe a person from the moment of conception until the moment of death, we can see the many changes in reality that had to take place during its lifetime. We can see the whole transformation as a single event, or we can see it happening from second to second, in imperceptibly subtle changes. It would be an impossible task to point out which actual moment within that person's life was the *real* moment. This is because each moment, is just as important and real as all other moments, to the fabric of time. We cannot exclude even one single moment, because it took the aggregation of every single moment to make up the completed lifetime.

It could be said that creation manifested instantaneously in relation to infinite time. That instant, compared with infinite time, can be stretched or reduced to any apparent length depending upon the viewpoint of the observer. In other words, in addition to our normal 3D time, there also exists within us another natural state of being that is outside of time. What we think of, as everyday time, is relative, while the other kind of time is universal.

This duality of time causes a split in our consciousness between the inner and outer selves. It is upon the universal desire to unite this diametrically opposed consciousness, and the acquisition and application of the knowledge to do so, that we will focus our attention.

Basic Dynamics of Time

To understand the dynamics of time, we need to have, at least, a minimal understanding of the multidimensional universe in which we live. We, as human beings, are currently concerned with at least five separate dimensions. We may think that we are not aware of some of them, but we work within them—or within reflections of them—all of the time. We are most aware of the Third Dimension because it is our physical universe we see all around us. This makes us three-dimensional beings. However, we are also aware of the Fourth Dimension, because we reflect it through our emotions. In addition, we experience a reflection of the Fifth Dimension with the "thinking" part of our minds.

Each dimension has its own kind of time. We are most familiar with three-dimensional time because we conduct our affairs by it. We are aware of the *Now*, the *Future* and the *Past*.

We experience "Present time " reality, as a continuous Now, that is constantly and instantaneously disengaging from the present. What was our present, becomes the past, while our subjective consciousness continues moving into what we perceive as the future, which constantly assumes a new position in the present. This is three-dimensional time. Notice that it only goes in the direction of the future, but is always the Now. In three-dimensional time we have no means of reclaiming the past, nor do we ever actually experience the future. Time for us is always the Present in forward motion.

Earth Cycles

Ever since we first stood erect and looked with beatific wonder at the sun, the moon and the stars, we have desired to master our environment. With the more complete knowledge of our metaphysical environment that is now available, we can begin to reshape our destiny, first from within us as a changing belief system, and secondly, externally in our environment as we begin to master time.

We no longer need to exist as human flotsam, drifting through life in benign ignorance. We, as potential time travelers, are in the process of discovering our immortality.

The following may seem rather complex and in violation of the letting-go principle of realizing what already is, but there comes a time when an exertion of will is necessary to bring about any kind of three-dimensional change. This is simply the nature of the 3D. We have not reached the point that we can just daydream reality into being, We need to do the footwork as well, whether it be pen to paper or hammer to nail.

Although a perfect reality already exists for us outside of linear time, in order for us to experience it, the inertia of the past has to be overcome. This entails the exertion of the Collective Will. Because you are part of this will, the Collective effort becomes part of what is called *Soul intent*, or *Creative intent*. In other words, a part of you must take creative action at a given time to bring about the necessary change for you.

Using the caterpillar-to-butterfly example, even though the caterpillar is already the butterfly in the purest sense, there comes a time of intense effort to bring about the change as the butterfly painfully emerges from its cocoon. Or, although within the seed there is the fruit bearing plant, there is a need for it to be planted and nurtured.

Chapter 5
Paradox

In Progress

As a fledgling Time Traveler, you are entering into what is called *in progress*. This means you will change a little everyday for the better. The changes are almost imperceptible at first, but become more noticeable as you progress. This is the beginning of what you have hoped and waited for on some level of your being, since the beginning of your sojourn into physical manifestation. It is a spectacular event that needs time to mature.

When you first created your *present time* on this time track you were unable to study the material in this book, because it did not exist then. The material contained here, was ultimately written by you, for you, from outside of time as you presently understand it. What is happening to you is utterly different than what happened to you on the original time track.

By no means an easy undertaking, you will need all of the help and encouragement you can get. This is the beginning for us. We are the pioneers that people a thousand years from now will be grateful to for having paved the way.

Tremendous Karma

Tremendous Karma in the form of magnetic force will try to pry you away from these studies in order to bring you back into the original time loop. These forces are neither good or evil. They are simply a built in maintenance system that mindlessly repairs and keeps your illusions in tact. We are in a Cosmic play pen spiraling around and around in the illusion of time. We have been doing this for a very long time, and without intervention, we will probably continue to do it for a very long time, possibly *forever*.

Lets continue our investigation of the Third Dimension. We need to delve into our 3D world a little more deeply so we can compare it with the Fourth Dimension.

In review, we established that the Third Dimension is outward facing, or six directions of out from a common center.

Contrary to beliefs held in this time period, ascending into higher levels of vibrations still belong to the realm of the Third Dimension and not the Fourth. This is because vibration as motion starts from the void in the First Dimension and accumulatively processes upward in vibration until the sum total of all vibration is accrued[1]. What we now think of as *forward time* is also the property of the Third Dimension—contrary to popular scientific opinion—and not to the Fourth Dimension which is backward or inward motion, *backward time*.

It is important that we establish the difference between the Third and Fourth Dimensions, because this was a major point of confusion for spiritual students during this time period. We stated previously, that the Fourth Dimension is equal and opposite to the Third Dimension. It is a mirror image in the purest sense. Every equal aspect is inside out, upside down, and backwards from one another. They perfectly counter balance each other. They are the two opposite halves of one thing. They are the same place from opposite view points.

A good example of this in our everyday world, is male and female. Another example of interaction with this principle, in Human Beings, is the right and left lobes of the brain.

A little time spent comparing elements of the Third and Fourth dimensions is in order at this point. These distinctions have to be absolutely *clear* before we can venture on to the Fifth Dimension.

We have established that the Third Dimension has six directions of out. This would mean that the Fourth Dimension would have to have six directions of *in*.

In summary, the Three Dimensional view point is from a single point to all directions of out. In order to simulate a 4D view point, we would have to establish a view point coming from everywhere, converging upon a single point. To help you do this, imagine yourself as coming from everywhere in space, looking inward toward a single point of white light at your very center. As you converge in upon this point from all directions, you are moving in a direction of *in*.

---

[1] For those of you who are students of Astrology, this outward motion was understood by the Ancients as the fundamental nature of *Aries*, color red, which represents the Third Dimension as forward or outward motion.

Chapter 6

Introduction to the Dynamics of Time

At the very beginning of this creative cycle, at the moment of Creation, all that came into being was created perfectly. Creation has no other choice than to be perfect. The puzzle is created by the pieces, and the pieces are each created by the puzzle. Perfection is an amazingly dynamic, ever changing state, rather than the static unchanging state of being that is usually ascribed to it. The problem is, although creation happened instantaneously, there is a relative time factor inherent within that instant. The instant of time it took for creation to achieve a state of perfection, has become all of time as we normally perceive it. That instant, relative to infinite time, can be virtually any length, depending upon the viewpoint of the observer.

Multidimensional Universe

In order to understand the dynamics of time, we need to have, at least, a minimal understanding of the multidimensional universe we live in. We as human beings, are at present, concerned with at least five separate dimensions. We may think that we are not aware of some of them, but we actually work within them—or reflections of them—all of the time.

To reiterate we are most aware of the Third Dimension because it is our physical universe we see all around us. This makes us, basically, three dimensional beings. However, we are also aware of the Fourth Dimension, because it is reflected through our emotions. A reflection of the Fifth Dimension is experienced with our minds.

Each dimension has its own time. We are most familiar with three dimensional time, because we conduct our affairs by it. We are aware of the Now, the Future and the Past. As was stated in Chapter 4, present time reality—as a continuous Now—becomes the past as it moves into the future, and assumes a new position for us, in the present. This is three dimensional time. Notice that it only goes in the direction of the future, but is always the Now. In three dimensional time, we have no means of reclaiming the past, nor do we ever actually experience the future. Time for us, is always the Present, in forward motion.

The Fourth Dimension is an emotional and spiritual labyrinth for us, and is in every way, equal and opposite to the Third Dimension. One of those opposites, is time. Where the Third Dimension moves into the future, the Fourth Dimension retreats into the past.

An Avatar-less Age

Contrary to popular millenarianism beliefs[1], the Age we are about to begin, is Avatar-less (Leaderless) in that the return of the Christ is in mass and as such, is a lesson that must be learned individually. This is the reason that no man can predict the exact time of His return, because it is different for each individual. And is also the reason so many people believe that they are Jesus.

---

[1] The belief in the impending return of Jesus, and a thousand years of enlightenment, known as the *Millennium*, or *Golden Age*.

CHAPTER 7

THE PRIMORDIAL DIMENSIONS

Our goal is God consciousness. It is comprised of all other consciousness in perfect balance. But, what does this mean? What exactly is God consciousness?

The Inherent Qualities of God Consciousness

1. Omniscience—All-knowing.

2. Omnipresence—Being everywhere all at once.

3. Omnipotence—all-powerful.

Within God consciousness is something called Christ consciousness. It is the quality of God consciousness as an ever increasing capacity for universal love, which is ecstasy in motion and the interaction between two or more Beings. There exists a law of Order as regards attaining God consciousness. These are listed below.

Law of Order:

1. The establishment of Cosmic consciousness in the current incarnation.

2. Conscious contact with our *Time Traveling Oversoul* from outside of linear 3D time.

3. The birth of Christ consciousness within the safe and protected environment of Cosmic consciousness.

4. And finally, to begin to realize and manifest God consciousness here in the third dimension.

As we progress through the Chapters, we will examine each of the components of God consciousness.

In this Chapter we are going to look much deeper into the three dimensions that comprise the third dimension, but first a little spiritual stretching exercise is in order.

OK, Who Did It?

Have you ever wondered about how existence began? If things are in existence, did they come from something? Where did that something come from? We are told that it all sprang into existence from nothingness. What is nothingness, where did it come from, and how did something come from it? We are told that it all came from a pinpoint of super condensed matter in the form of a *Big Bang*.

Where did the pin point of super condensed matter come from? We are told that the universe is somewhere between ten and thirty billion years old, less than a nanosecond in relation to infinity. Why, in all of infinite time did the universe come into creation now? We are told that Man is not meant to know the answers to these riddles, and therefore cannot fathom the Universe with his limited mind. Where did that limitation in thinking come from? Who are we? What are we? Where is it all going?

Just a scant three hundred years ago, you might have been branded as a heretic for just asking such questions, let alone trying to answer them. What is wrong with trying to answer these kinds of questions? Why does it seem ridiculously impossible for us to even try? Is it that our minds are so limited that we cannot try, or is it that our minds are actually unlimited, and that artificial limitations have, somehow, been placed upon them? If artificial limitations have been placed upon our minds, what is the nature of the limitations, and who or what placed them there and how can they be removed or modified? What is our true potential and how can we access it now?

In our quest for an understanding of the multidimensional universe we live in, perhaps a logical place to start would be at the beginning of the current creative cycle. In order to begin to understand the concepts of creation, we need to ask two basic questions. The first question is, "How can something come from nothing?".

The second question is "What is nothing?". We can begin to examine the idea of nothing by first defining it. *Nothing* is the absence of *something*. Let us use the void of outer space as an example. We will, for simplicity's sake, remove all matter from it—including molecular, atomic, and subatomic structures—which leaves us with the blackness of infinite *space*. We now have an instance of what could be defined as nothingness.

However, far from being nothing, what we have defined is actually an unmeasurable example of *something*. To understand what I mean by this, let us redefine *nothingness* from a little different approach. If we can acknowledge that three-dimensional space is a place with a purpose in which things can (and do) happen, and by that definition, exists as part of the universal plan of things, then the *void*, or *empty space*, could be considered a *thing*, rather than *nothing*.

If three-dimensional space is *something*, then a true *void*, or actual *nothingness*, would exclude three-dimensional space, and preclude any kind of manifestation whatsoever. This means that *space*, as we know it, must exist in such a way as to displace or circumvent actual nothingness. In other words, *space* or the infinite *void*, is actually a place filled with an invisible something that cannot be measured. Considering that without it, all that we know as our universe could not exist, is testimony enough for its existence, whether we can measure it or not.

Ether Anyone?

The reason for the foregoing, is the reestablishment of a universal medium that is absolutely fundamental to Metaphysics. It has had many names in the past, but for the sake of simplicity, lets call it the *Ether*. This is a familiar term that is found in your dictionary. Below is a partial definition out of *The American Heritage Electronic Dictionary*.

> *Ether*. An all-pervading, infinitely elastic, mass-less medium formerly postulated as the medium of propagation of electromagnetic waves.

Notice the words, *formerly postulated*. This means the Scientists of this time period discounted the Ether as being unmeasurable, and therefore nonexistent. In other words, if I can't bite it and make it holler, it doesn't exist.

Just a Cosmic Kind of Guy

We exist in what is known as the Third Dimension, but how would a Cosmic Conscious Being view this? We know that the third dimension has height, breadth and width. This means we have access to, up and down (height), forwards and backwards (breadth), and side to side (width). It is the combination of the 1st, 2nd and 3rd dimensions that make up the complete Third Dimension. By the same token, we can assume that the Second Dimension is made up of a combination of the 1st and 2nd dimensions.

Looking through the eyes of a Cosmic conscious Being, what would the universe look like, and how different would it be from the way we perceive it? A Cosmic Conscious Being might view the universe in terms of multiple dimensions, which is utterly different than the way we view it. If this is true, then he would be able to see into the various super dimensions and inner space as easily as we see into the 3D. Not only could he perceive the separate dimensions, but he would be able to experience them as separate independent places as well, in the much same way we experience our three dimensions.

Let us travel with him instantaneously in his mind, to a time before this creative cycle, to view primordial energy in its most basic form. Remember that he has access to many more dimensions then we do, at least six, and possibly as many as twelve.

Let us travel with our hypothetical Cosmic conscious Time Traveler as he travels back billions of years into the past, and watch through his eyes, and understand through his mind, as he examines the primordial universe in its earliest moments in this creative cycle.

He would see the *First dimension*, as the birth place of all other dimensions. He would understand that here, energy exists as an infinite, or immeasurable point of nothingness. He would also see that there is another place called the *Second dimension* that is a universe of white light.

Here he can observe an infinite or immeasurable point of white light. He knows that the positive and negative poles exist in the same one dimensional space, but at alternating times. By our standards, this would be equivalent to something coming from nothing, but from the view point of a Cosmic Conscious Being, nothingness would simply appear as pure energy stored in the First dimension, from which springs all that we know and experience in our 3D universe. To him, the First dimension has always existed in a state of perpetual present timelessness.

Polarized Energy

A simpler way of stating this is, there exists polarized energy that alternates between the positive and negative poles of existence. When it is realized as the positive pole, it is in a state of maximum excitation.

When it is realized as the negative pole, it is in a vibration-less state. Technically each of these states individually are one dimensional. It is only when we expand our view point to include both polar opposites at the same time, do we perceive the Second Dimension.

To visualize something as alien as an infinite point, is most likely very difficult for the average three dimensional mind. So, at this time, it is sufficient to say that it is a point, and that it is infinite. There is nowhere in the First Dimension that it is not, and yet, it has no three-dimensional or measurable space to it. It is therefore eternal or exists without beginning or end. Although it is a point, it gives the illusion of infinite three dimensional space.

This—the First Dimension—holds or creates space within actual nothingness that "exists" (does not exist) outside of space. The point of energy and space contained in the negative pole is *all* of the energy and space available to us in our universe.

As we watch, we see that this same energy in its excited state—in the positive pole of the Second dimension as white light—is the foundation for all of the *matter* available to us in our universe.

Following the viewpoint of our Cosmic Conscious Being, we next observe the creation of the Primordial Third dimension. If we examine the two states of being in the Second dimension, we see that there is energy, either vibrating at a maximum rate, or not vibrating at all. After all, it is the same energy in the same space. The mechanics of vibration oscillate back and forth between black and white. It takes time to do this. Although it appears instantaneous in the Second dimension, there is, what an Electronic Engineer might refer to as a propagation delay. In other words, even instantaneous takes time to happen. It is within this instant that the field of creation, comes into being!

What Did He Say?

The mechanics of the time delay between white and black, show white light disassembling into the components of the spectrum. Each vibrationally separate component can be experienced as a separate two dimensional universe, occupying the *same* space at *separate* times.

As we have seen, there are three distinct phases concerning the Primordial Universe. The three phases are summed up below:

The Primordial First Dimension

The minimum phase is energy at rest. It is the absolute negative pole of existence, and is part of the vibrational sequence, even though it is absent of vibration. It is a place of never ending experienceless-ness. It is a universe of blackness, it is called the Primordial First dimension, and is the birth place of the Sun sign *Sagittarius*. In our three dimensional world, we know it as *space*. Each dimension has its own kind of time. The Primordial First dimension is the *Primoridal Past*[1]

The Primordial Second Dimension

The maximum phase, is energy at its maximum state of vibration. It is the sum of all vibratory states. It is a universe of white light. It is—by its self—a one dimensional universe, but because of its polarization with the negative pole, exists in two dimensional space. This is the Primordial Second dimension, it is the primary universal center and is the birth place of the Sun Sign *Leo*[2]. The Second dimension, in our three dimensional world, represents all that is in existence, that resides within the void. In other words, all created matter in any form, within space.

The Primordial Second dimension is the *Primoridal Present*[3] in that it can never experience anything other than itself, in present time, and it can never cease to exist. Remember this, because it is one of the keys to immortality.

The Primordial Third Dimension

The transitory phase is also the sum of all vibratory states, but divided into separate components. Although the sum of its components is white light, and the absence of its components is blackness, white and black are not available within the transitory phase.

The 3rd dimension—that is the singular 3rd dimension, as distinguished from the composite Third dimension, which is made up from the 1st, 2nd, and 3rd Dimensions—represents all that moves or has outward motion. It is a universe of rainbows, and is the birth place of the Sun Sign *Aries*. The Primordial Third dimension, because of its

---

[1] Time before time.

[2] The Primordial Second dimension is the stellar prototype, or Universal Sun.

[3] Time of forever *now*.

forward motion, is the *Primordial Future*[4].

Let us see if we can simplify this a little. When we view our three dimensional universe, we see that the starry world and the planets are
suspended in space, and that they have motion. We can say that the
space[5] belongs to the 1st dimension. Next we can say that everything
else belongs to the 2nd dimension as centers of matter, and because
of the lack of motion, is timeless. And finally, we can say that everything that moves belongs to the 3rd dimension. Because everything
that belongs to the 2nd dimension also has the potential of motion,
means that the contents of the 2nd and 3rd dimensions are exactly the
same, except that the Third dimension places the added dimension of
actualized *motion*, and the resultant three dimensional *time*. This is
an important difference between the Time Travelers philosophy concerning *time*, and current models of the universe where the Fourth
dimension provides *time*.

In the next Chapter, we will continue with the exploration of the
various *dimensions* and how they relate to consciousness.

---

[4] Time of cycles.

[5] Includes all space—even the space between the atoms within your body.

CHAPTER 8

IMMEDIATE AND LONG TERM GOALS

What Are Our Goals?

1. Short Term—Our short term goal is to merge our conscious view points from the Third and Fourth dimensions to fully realize the Fifth dimension.

2. Interim Term—Our interim term goals are to realize Cosmic consciousness in the Sixth dimension and to prepare a "time portal" within our consciousness for the arrival of our Time Traveling Oversoul.

3. Long Term—Our long term goal of attaining God Consciousness, and manifesting it here in the third dimension, is an ongoing process. There are virtually an infinite number of levels in God Consciousness. However, there is a minimal level that can be called God Consciousness. Levels below this are not concerned with God Consciousness, and are but sub-levels.

Intent of the Creative Will

It is my belief, and the crux of Time Travelers philosophy, that the intent and desire of the Creative Will, is to manifest *God consciousness* here in the Third dimension. From the dimensions outside of the Third dimension there is a lack of detail, like extreme near sightedness. Abstraction without specifics. The 3D lends the necessary corrective lenses needed to complete our ability to see.

I am convinced that the Third dimension is the Creator's crowning achievement. I have glimpsed it in, what I call, its perfected state, where we are all *One* and yet *separate*, where we are so filled with loving wonder that it almost hurts, where each moment is delicious beyond comprehension, and yet, so familiar and so expected.

In this next section we will begin to examine the various kinds of consciousness. This is necessary in order to help you begin to understand how you are constructed, in the belief that knowledge is power and the road to enlightenment.

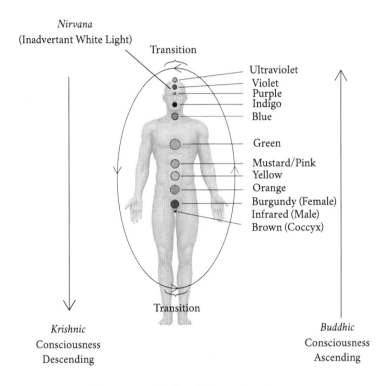

Figure 8.1: Cycle of Conscious States

Notice in *Figure 8.1* that the flow of experience is locked into a circle or spiral. Ascending vibrational energy (Female) is represented by Buddhic consciousness, while descending vibrational energy (Male) is represented by Krishnic consciousness. The traveling center of consciousness, considered as the *Self* or *Personality*, is about the size of a ping-pong ball and travels with great difficulty[1] through the successive vibrational centers known as chakras.

There is no real love involved with either Buddhic or Krishnic consciousness, as found in Christ Consciousness, except on a personal possessive level[2]. The key elements here are personal power, wisdom, temporary states of bliss, and detached compassion. The misconception is that *Nirvana*—used here to mean existing in a "white-light state of exultation"—is reached and maintained by ascending in vibration to the *Third Eye*[3]. That this much sought after state can be reached and experienced as "white light" is certainly true, and one of the fundamental tenets of Time Travelers philosophy, but that it can be maintained on a permanent basis in this manner, is absolutely false.

Due to the inevitable "flywheel" effect, this state cannot be maintained and results in a state of consciousness called *Buddhas of compassion*, which unbeknown to the student is the beginning of Krishnic consciousness.

Krishnic consciousness is one of giving of one's self absolutely without regard for personal consequences. It almost always results in martyrdom in extreme cases. The student never realizes what is wrong (God, why hast thou forsaken me?). Christ consciousness, on the other hand, is the result of the student realizing that traveling around in circles or spirals will never get anywhere. This realization usually takes the Soul a considerable number of life-times. The merging and transcendence of both Buddhic and Krishnic consciousness, results in a centering. A move from the outside of consciousness, to the internalized being-ness of it. This is the first level of two levels of Christ consciousness.

However, the first level of Christ Consciousness presents many dangers including death for the unsuspecting student. This conscious-

---

[1] This effort is usually reserved for dedicated monks or mystics, and is rarely observed in the average person.

[2] It is interesting to note that the word *love* has crept into the language of some western Buddhist's writings.

[3] A center of consciousness found just above and between the physical eyes.

ness is associated with unprepared neophytes that rush in where fools fear to tread. Being a pure positive force, it drives the environment negative. This is the path of the Saints most of whom were martyred. Jesus was executed at 33. The lessons he laid down as a world teacher, and Avatar for the Age, made it possible for us to avoid most of the pitfalls associated with this level.

Many Time Travelers are and will be returning from the future to manifest in previous incarnations. The Time Traveling Oversoul actually exists temporarily outside of Three dimensional linear time, in something called *non-linear time*. If it approaches a previous incarnation which is not sufficiently prepared, the approach can drive the inherent personality or ego, within that incarnation into an out of balance condition called the Messiah complex, whereby the personality believes that he or she is the Christ. This would be wonderful if it were actually true, but unfortunately, this is a manifestation of the what is being called the *False Christ*, which is an extremely out of balance condition in consciousness. Avoidance of this undesirable condition can be had if certain steps are taken[4].

Cosmic consciousness is the apex of what could be called the *Anti-Christ*. It is everything that the Christ is not, and nothing, of what, the Christ is. It is equal and opposite to the Christ in every way. Perfect mirror images. Cosmic consciousness brings with it perfect knowledge of the Universal, whereas the Christ brings with it perfect knowledge of the perfect self.

In Cosmic consciousness the student has overcome all of the Satanic and Demonic forces that compose this consciousness. Although temporary states of ecstasy and personal power are part of the natural emotional/spiritual makeup of Cosmic consciousness, they should be avoided, as it can become a powerful and unnecessary distraction, if not an addiction.

The major role for Cosmic consciousness, once it is attained, is to provide a safe and balanced platform for the newly forming Christ consciousness. There are many continuous progressive levels of inward expansion (or relaxation) of Cosmic consciousness (polymorphic), whereas Christ consciousness is a continuous outward expansion (Uni-morphic). Their homogenized and balanced mergence is the beginning of actual *God Consciousness*.

---

[4] These steps are carefully explained later in the Course.

There are many levels of God Consciousness below the level mentioned above, while still called God Consciousness, these levels, although incomplete, are indications of the particular path the student has taken. It is important to denote this distinction because there is a great difference between actual God Consciousness, and those lesser states by the same name.

Dangers Related to Manifesting the First Level of Christ Consciousness

As was stated above, manifesting Christ Consciousness is a two part process. The problem with manifesting Christ Consciousness is that it is extremely dangerous. Not only from a physical aspect (Jesus only lasted three years), but can be disastrous on the spiritual level as well. This is not for spiritual babies to play around with. We are unleashing the unlimited side of our nature, and without safeguards there can be unlimited problems.

It takes a perfectly balanced combination of Cosmic consciousness and Christ consciousness to realize God Consciousness. To simply manifest Christ Consciousness without the protection and balance of Cosmic Consciousness, is far too dangerous for us to consider. The Souls who are foolish enough to attempt it are immediately caught up in a kind of divine paranoia that is very hard to break out of. We can observe this in the many Messiahs that are beginning to show up.

CHAPTER 9

OPENING THE HEART, THROAT AND UPPER SOLAR PLEXUS

Let is take a break from our studies, and begin learning how to open up various energy centers known as chakras. We will start by concentrating on opening and warming up the Heart center located in the middle of the chest at the sternum, and not the actual area where the physical heart is located. To find it, feel for the indentation located between the breasts[1].

We need to learn and practice these beginning techniques on a daily basis to prepare us for the Fifth Dimensional Meditations later on, which are absolutely necessary to progress in this course. For most of us, this shouldn't take more than five minutes a day to soon become proficient.

Our next step after opening the heart center, is exchanging energies between the throat and solar plexus. Attention must be paid to the order in which the steps are taken.

Order in Which the Steps Must be Taken

1. A centering process has to take place to bring you into the heart center. This can be accomplished through stimulation of the heart center by rubbing it in a circular motion with the finger tips of one of your hands[2]. Do this until you can feel some heat begin to generate there. It might also help to visualize a middle, to light green flower that is opening. With practice it can feel quite warm if not hot. If you do not feel warmth right away, this is OK. It will come with time.

2. Switch hands so the finger tips of your non-dominant hand are on the upper portion of your solar plexus. This helps to secure the progress made there. With your dominant hand place your finger tips at your throat center, just below the Adam apple, so the fingers are together and pointing towards the throat. Now begin to slowly open your fingers as you visualize your throat

---

[1] If a physical handicap is preventing you from doing these exercisers, mentally visualize doing them.

[2] I use a counterclockwise motion, but you might find clockwise better for you.

chakra begin to open. See this center as a mid range blue flower blooming. As it opens, you may feel a warm rush of energy in the solar plexus. If you do do not, this is OK. It helps if you can generate energy at your finger tips. Do this by visualizing and feeling energy charging up at your finger tips. Visualize its color as bluish white.

CHAPTER 10

OPENING THE MOUTH AND LOWER SOLAR PLEXUS CENTERS

In this Chapter we are going to learn how to open up the next pair of Centers, but first, I invite you to look at *Figure 10.1* and *Figure 10.2* which show the basic differences between men and women. Although men and women have the same number of chakras located in the same areas of the body, the chart shows the preferences between male and female. This—in part—explains some of the more obvious differences between us.

I know there is a lot of information contained on *Figure 10.1*, but for now just note the basic differences between a man and woman. Don't worry about learning everything on the chart at this point in your studies. We will get into a detailed study of the various Centers and colors, and what they mean, in a later lesson.

The next figure, *Figure 10.2*, shows a little different representation of the basic differences between a man and a woman. This is in the purest most abstract sense, and is not meant as an actual representation of the human aura. Keep in mind that both men and women have the identical number of chakras, but prefer the combinations shown here. The actual size shape and colors radiating in the human aura depends upon many factors, and may change from moment to moment depending upon the emotional/mental content.

Meditation Review

1. Place the finger tips of your dominant hand[1] on top of the upper portion of your solar plexus, located about two inches above the navel. Visualize it relaxing and becoming receptive. Feel it slowly opening like a dark yellow or golden flower if you are a male. If you are female, visualize it as a bright pink flower. It helps me to make a slow opening motion with my finger tips. When you have done this, go to the next step.

---

[1] (Right hand if you are right handed, and left hand if you are left handed.

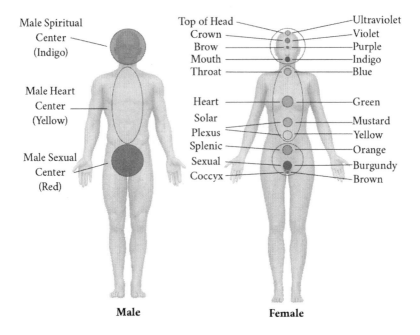

Figure 10.1: Basic Differences Between Men and Women

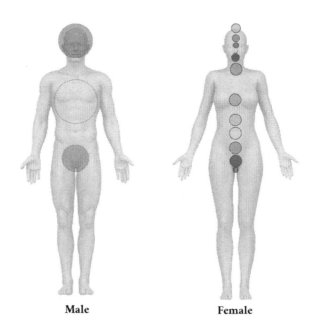

Figure 10.2: Basic Differences Between Men and Women

In this meditation technique, we are going to open two more balanced chakras, the Mouth-center (Indigo) and the lower half of the solar plexus (Bright yellow)

Opening the Mouth and Lower Solar Plexus:

1. In each of these exercises try to generate energy at your finger tips. Always begin by warming up the Heart-center. This can be done by rubbing in a circular motion. Also by picturing a green flower opening up. Next, activate the Throat-center by tapping it and visualizing it opening up like a blue flower. You can also use the energy of your dominant hand (fingers together pointing in towards the throat) by slowly opening this center with an opening motion of the fingers (fingers together pointing towards the Throat-center, slowly spread the finger tips away from each other in a widening circle). Feel the energy in your finger tips open this center.

2. Open the *Upper Solar Plexus-center* using the same process and visualizing a pink or dark yellow flower. Feel the Upper Solar Plexus as an empty vessel waiting to be filled by the energy from the Throat-center. Both the Throat and Upper Solar Plexus may begin to feel warm with varying degrees of elation. If you still feel nothing, don't be discouraged. The exercises will help you whether you feel immediate results or not. This help will come in the form of improved relationships and circumstances in your everyday world.

3. Use the same process to open the *Mouth-center* (Indigo, a very dark blue purple), and the *Lower Solar Plexus center* (Bright yellow). Tap your lips lightly to wake up this center, then using the opening motion with your finger tips, slowly open your mouth at the same time. Once done, switch hands, and use the opening motion on the lower solar plexus, located just below the navel. If this center is slow to respond, use the circular rubbing motion outlined for the Heart-center. Feel and visualize this center relaxing and slowly opening. This may cause a feeling of warmth from your throat, extending all the way down to the lower solar plexus.

Chapter II

The Twelve Faces of God

Beginning Time Travel & Remote Viewing Techniques

So many people have asked me to give a clear and simple instruction on how to do Remote Viewing using Time Travel Techniques. The following is as simple and clear as I can make it.

Time travel is usually associated with physically traveling into the past or the future, with all of its attendant problems, such as meeting yourself or what would happen to you if you killed your grandfather? However these are the product of three dimensional thinking. Time travel, as I understand it and have experienced it, is possible because of the nature of time and the fact that we are already everywhere at the same time. We could say that there is only one universal consciousness manifesting in everyone, and the way we experience time allows us to experience ourselves as separate individuals touching momentarily on the physical level.

Remote Viewing

The ability to penetrate the illusion of time, allows one to be able to experience time as a single simultaneous event. The consequence of non-linear time enables a person to be able to experience any time frame he chooses, whether past, present or future[1]. To be able to do this kind of Remote Viewing takes some practice to become confident.

It is important to know when you are actually Remote Viewing, and not simply day dreaming. We use our ordinary senses brought together to form a sharp point that is able to pierce the three dimensional protective sheath. A great deal of what is used (after that) is focused visualization, which is in the realm of creative imagination.

The Astral Tube

Remote Viewing, or previously known as *Clairvoyance*, is certainly not new. Many students of metaphysics, and advanced mystics, could

---

[1] The *future*, because every event that ever will happen has already happened in non-linear time.

"see" at a distance. One such method is by erecting what is called an *Astral Tube* while in Open Eye Meditation[2].

Whirlpool

If I wish to examine an event, I visualize a whirlpool, about a foot across[3]. Next, I try to see down the tube to a predetermined place, person or object. This method takes some practice, but allows the practitioner to get a clear picture of what they wish to see.

Psychic Attack

I had studied this very method, only I used it for healing rather than trying to harm someone. I sat down and began to meditate. I erected a whirlpool to see if I could track down whoever was doing this to me. At first I couldn't see anything but black. But then, suddenly, I saw the Hatha Yoga teacher sitting in a lotus position. My view was from above and behind her, but I immediately recognized her.

Her intensity was strong and destructive, and it all was aimed at me. I had been teaching my students about a psychic defense technique, utilizing the mental construction of a mirror.

The Mirror

The point of the lesson was to erect a mirror in front of you when you felt that you were being attacked. I erected the mirror, and the attack stopped instantly. I found out that the poor woman had to go to bed for several days. In the next meeting where she was attending, she followed me around like a puppy. It is an old occult maxim that "an ounce of defense is worth a pound of offense".

Simple Instructions

One must be aware of the distinction between time travel, and astral projection. Astral projection, or its cousin, Etheric projection, are about traveling in your astral or etheric bodies, to experience or examine the Astral Planes, or the Etheric Planes. These bodies—the lower and upper etheric—are part of the physical complex, interpenetrating the physical body, which allows you to be able to experience our physical earthly existence.

---

[2] See Chapter 1.

[3] My whirlpool is usually clockwise.

Remote Viewing, using Time travel techniques, utilizes some of the techniques that are used to facilitate astral and etheric projection, however, the similarities end there. Time travel has its own set of rules, which need to be known before attempting to experience a time traveling event. Although the rules are simple, the disregarding of them will most likely prevent you from achieving non-linear time, where true time travel is possible. Once having achieved non-linear time, what follows is relatively safe and easy. I have listed the three most important rules below.

Three Rules

1. Fear—Fear is the greatest deterrent to time travel, and facing the unknown is one of the main reasons for fear. The reason for the detailed examination of the unknown in the *A Course in Time Travel*, is the thought that if one is well informed about the unknown, then the unknown becomes known, and is no longer fear producing. The bottom line is, if you are afraid, then your chances of time traveling are very slim. If you find that you are afraid when attempting to access non-linear time, I would suggest studying the material that is available here on the Time Travelers web site, until you feel that, through a greater understanding of the unknown, you are no longer afraid.

2. Permission—This may sound strange that you need permission, but it is very important to ask permission of your Inner Being. The heart of Time Travelers is to make available vital information about your Time Traveling Oversoul (TTO), so that you might facilitate the necessary link up with it. Since your TTO already has access to non-linear time, it makes sense that you should avail yourself to it in order to learn. Believe me when I say that nothing in life is more important than gaining attention from your TTO.

3. Persistence—Without persistence and a great deal of patience, you are probably not yet spiritually mature enough to convince your TTO to bother with you. When you are ready to make a commitment, instead of just pursuing a fun ride, then your TTO will be more than willing to help you. It is, after all, you from the remote future, and uniting with you is very important for its personal evolution.

A Simple Method

Here is a simple exercise you can use to begin Remote Viewing. While seated comfortably, think about the room in which you are seated. In your mind, see the room as clearly as you can. Let's say that you are in your front room, visualize the larger objects, like a table or a chair. Visualize yourself moving over to the table. Look at the items on the table top. Try to remember exactly what was placed there. If you can't remember, get up and look at the items on the table top, and then try the exercise again. Visualize yourself moving over to the table. If there is a picture in the room, look at it closely, and visualize who is in the picture. Next, move over to a piece of furniture. Imagine that you are running your hand over it. How does it feel? Is it rough or smooth? While imagining this, look at your hands. Try to imagine how your hands look. Next, move to where your body is located. Imagine that you can see yourself. Watch yourself breath. Do you look peaceful?

Practice the above technique until you feel that you can actually begin to see what you are imagining. Once you have a little experience doing this, you might try the next exercise. Although some of you will recognize this as *Etheric Projection*, I offer it as a way to gain confidence. As you begin to master one technique, other techniques will intrigue you.

A More Advanced Method

Find a comfortable spot to sit where you won't be disturbed. It is better if you sit rather than lie down because the latter tends to produce sleep and dreams rather than actual time travel. Relax your mind and body as much as is possible without going to sleep. Begin by thanking your Inner Being for helping and guiding you[4]. Think about the place or person you wish to explore. See and feel yourself traveling easily to that time and place. Visualize the details of what you are seeing. Are there buildings or streets? See if you can read any signs, such as a street sign. Look at your hands, see if you can see them. Listen for any sounds, such as people talking. What are they saying? Begin to feel yourself there in the place. What form have you taken? Are you in a physical body? Is it male or female? Or are you sort of floating above the scene? Look for a newspaper. Look at the date. If it is tomorrows paper, try to remember what the headlines said. See if you can find a

---

[4] This method seems to work better than simply asking for help.

street sign. What is your sense of when it is? How are people dressed? Ask them questions. Listen for answers. See if you can locate and remember the winning lotto number (lol!).

It is very important to gain confidence that you are actually time traveling. If you are having difficulty achieving this technique, perhaps it is because you are trying too hard. Relax and just become an observer watching a movie. Have fun with it. Remember that others are doing it, and so can you.

Another Advanced Method

If you want to experience being a particular person, you need to focus upon that person until you can see and feel what that person was seeing and feeling. It is helpful to gather as much information about that person as possible. Sometimes while visiting a time or place, you may find yourself experiencing someone you are not familiar with. This person is probably a karmic self of yours[5].

I would recommend, at first, to pick someone famous. Find out all that you can about the person, and then meditate upon the time and place where you want to have your experience. This is so much more informative than reading a book about the person.

Practice, Practice, Practice!

At first it may seem difficult to see anything, but with practice things will begin to easily come into focus. Have fun with it. See if you can find out something that can be verified in present time. The main difference between time traveling and day dreaming is that a time traveling event has a life of its own. By this I mean that you are more of an observer rather than a creator. In a day dream you can change things around to suit you. When time traveling, one usually cannot.

My Personal Favorite Methods

I have refined the method I use, over quite a few years, but it wasn't until these last few years that I have paid attention to exactly *how* I do it. I find that sitting in a recliner, with my eyes open or closed and concentrate upon what I wish to see, seems to work well for me. I have been re-examining the earliest period of the creative cycle, so I will use that as an example.

---

[5] Even though we are each everyone, there are some incarnations that are more directly tied to us than others.

Learn to Relax

I relax my body and mind as much as I am able. This step is important for me to do, so I would suggest that you spend some time relaxing also. This is easy for me because I have been doing this kind of meditation for a long time.

In my minds eye, I imagine a glimmer of a black speck that is without dimension. I "know" that I am observing the exact beginning moment in the creative cycle. This part of time travel seems to be automatic[6].

Although it is devoid of light, I can see it clearly. I hold this sight in my mind for as long as it takes to find out exactly how the creative cycle unfolds from this state of existence, to the next. Sometimes I will get a flash of understanding, which is then automatically verbalize into words. I believe that each object I study has its own built-in detailed description, available to anyone able to access it.

As I watch intently, I see this black speck beginning to change states. It seems to "crack", or fragment into an evenly divided matrix of innumerable seemingly identical crystalline parts. As I watch, I begin to understand what is happening. Each crystalline piece looks identical to every other piece, however, I "know" that each crystal is as different as snow flakes, where no two crystals are identical. I "know" that what I am observing is the creation of space and multiple dimensions. I watch it just as though I were watching a video on T.V. Sometimes I have watched a certain process for hundreds of times before I was finally able to understand what it was and how it worked.

Many nights I will, as soon as I get into bed, close my eyes, and immediately concentrate upon whatever I wish to see. Another favorite time for me to Time Travel is when I first awaken in the morning. The method I most commonly use at present, is to visualize, as I write or type, translating what I am viewing into sound using my voice, and then into the written word.

Using Open Eye Meditation

Whatever or whomever you wish to study or experience, requires the ability to focus and concentrate. This is very important. If you have

---

[6] This is why, in *Remote Viewing*, a person can go unerringly to a place, simply by being given a series of numbers, the meaning of which is unknown to the person, which is a code for that particular place.

an undisciplined mind, the inability to still your mind, then I would recommend practicing Open Eye Meditation. I developed this meditation especially for the purpose of stilling the mind while attempting to Time Travel.

Open Eye Meditation works simply because, when done correctly, it occupies both lobes of your brain, allowing you to be free of the constant interruption from that part of the mind. In addition to Open Eye Meditation, I have used, with great success, overloading my hearing by playing loud music through earphones. I found that "Trance" music occupied that portion of my mind, while Open Eye Meditation occupied another portion of my mind.

These methods may seem overly simplistic, but they work. However, I must warn you that for some, it will take many hours of practice on a daily basis before you gain confidence. If you are one of those people who wants everything immediately, you most likely won't have the patience required to master time traveling or remote viewing.

Although many of you will recognize some of these methods as the same methods used to Astral Project, I would recommend not projecting, for this is far too distracting to achieve a time travel state, at least at this tender stage in your development.

Gives you Omniscience & Omnipotence

Most of the Time Travelers text and diagrams come from the ability to Time Travel. I have studied each of the two thousand year Ages in the 26,000 year cycle of the earth, for an example, finding out amazing things far beyond our present abilities. This sort of omniscience was due entirely to the ability to time travel.

When I was writing the bulk of the Time Travelers text, I was seated in front of my computer, using a word processor program. I had on ear phones through which I played very loud techno and trance music. This seemed to occupy the noisy part of my brain. Using this method, I was able to write directly into the word processor what I was seeing and hearing. I, to the consternation of family and friends, would spend, sometimes, 18 hours a day, 6 or 7 days a week, for months. I never seemed to get hungry, or even thirsty. My family was afraid I was going to die before I was finished, and would make sure that I ate something, and drank, at least, water. I loved that stage of development, although I wouldn't want to have to do it again.

Hooking Up with your Oversoul

When I was first approach by my Time Traveling Oversoul, I was only 22 years old. That was in 1959. The introduction was in the form of a well modulated man's voice. After work each day, I would rush home, to hear more of what this man had to say. The first request given to me to accomplish was to stare at a spot of white light in my mind, with my eyes closed. The purpose of this exercise was to eventually be able to decode "white light"—which I have done—in order to decipher the *Solar Akasha*.

In the beginning, back when I was 22, I was very frustrated, when after six months of staring at a spot of white within my minds eye, had resulted in very little return. At least this is what I thought at the time. Now, I can look back and see how perfect it was to challenge me in this way. It wasn't until years later, when I discovered that the well modulated man's voice was me from my own future.

Your Progress

Since we each are as different as snow flakes, I know that each of us will be approached by our Time Traveling Oversoul in the best way for each person. How you progress, and what you develop into, may be entirely different from my development. Please remember that there is *nothing* more important then teaming up with your Oversoul. We all will take this step sooner or later. I preferred sooner.

Perhaps, when you are ready, your *Inner Being* will take you on a guided tour. Be patient, because, like anything in life worth mastering, Time Travel and Remote Viewing, takes time, discipline and effort. You must want this more than anything in life. At least, this is how it has affected me. And have *fun* with it. I am just as excited today about time travel as I was when I was 22.

Chapter 12
Opportunities

Human thought seems to manifest in quantum leaps. A period of time transpires where little or no original thought occurs. Then for no apparent reason tremendous progress in thought begins to happen. It might come from a single individual or a group or groups. It might come through a single source such as music or science or through a broad spectrum of disciplines. Then just as suddenly as it started it stops.

As Time Travelers we are participating in the beginning of one of these quantum leaps. If we can fully grasp the meaning of this surge of understanding we, like surfers on an endless wave, will have the potential of forever riding the leading edge of new thought. This is an amazingly exciting potential, and one I would loath to miss. To be a part of such a golden opportunity, no amount of effort or sacrifice could possibly be considered too much. Opportunities like these are extremely rare and must be seized with both hands when such an occurrence does finally arise.

How many times has opportunity knocked on your door only to find you unwilling to take advantage of it? A fact that you later regretted? Life has a way of quickly passing. By the time we understand this it is too late. It is a sad fact that the average person in this time period has little chance of awakening. We exist in a catatonic morass of habits and routines. So buried are we in our daily life that we fail to notice that we have fallen sound asleep, nor are we able to notice that our friends and neighbors have fallen asleep as well. There may be moments that we awaken and vow to stay awake, but the next time we notice, it is decades later and much too late to do anything about it.

Unable to any longer amuse ourselves, we need to be constantly entertained lest we go mad from boredom. We exalt those who successfully entertain us, with riches and fame, and punished those who tried but failed.

CHAPTER 13

INTERCONNECTEDNESS AND NEXT LEVEL OF MEDITATION

There is an interconnectedness between the nature of white light, the centers within the human body, the Signs of the zodiac, the order of the Ages, and, in fact, the Solar System itself. *Figure 13.1* and *Figure 13.2* emphasize this interconnectedness.

According to Time Travelers texts, the Dark Ages consist of the three components of Aries (red), which are the three Earth Signs: Taurus, Virgo and Capricorn. These three Signs represent the three physical dimensions composing the Third dimension.

The Three Component Signs of Aries:

1. Taurus, as the 1st dimension (brown) is associated with our physical meat-body, and with the chakra at the coccyx center.

2. Virgo, as the 2nd dimension (burgundy) is associated with the indwelling consciousness of the physical personality, and the female sexual center.

3. Capricorn, as the 3rd dimension (orange) is the vitality that enables us to have life and motion in the 3rd dimension.

We are at a null point now between Virgo and Capricorn. The higher orange vibrations are already being felt by most sensitive people. It brings with it an overwhelming compulsion to *do*.

In *Figure 13.1*, notice that each of the three *Fire Signs*—Aries, Leo and Sagittarius—form a trinity descending from white light. Each of these in turn, are sub-divided into three Signs. Aries, as we discussed above, is divided into the three earth signs—Taurus, Virgo, and Capricorn. These four form the *Physical Ages* known as the Dark Ages in which we now find ourselves. Next is Leo, with its three subdivisions—Gemini, Libra and Aquarius. These four form the *Mental Ages*. The last Fire Sign is Sagittarius and its three sub-divisions—Cancer, Scorpio and Pisces—which form the *Spiritual Ages*.

This is a completely different order than that believed by modern astrologers. I believe this revised order is how the Ancients saw it. The current order is a serious mistake made by the Greeks who tried

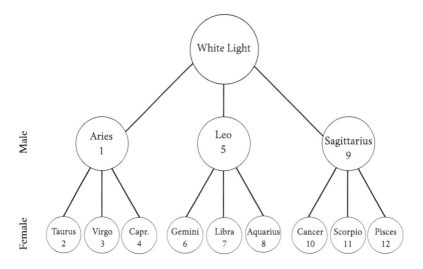

Figure 13.1: Relationship Bewteen Signs of the Zodiac and the Ages

to make the order of the Ages correspond to the same order that works for our Birth Signs. If the order of the Ages I am proposing is correct, and I think you will agree with me the it makes much more sense than the old order, then the *New millennium* we have just entered is the Age of Capricorn, and not the Age of Aquarius (see *Figure 13.2*).

Next Level of Meditation

In this meditation, we are going to open two more balanced chakras, the *Between the Eyes* chakra, sometimes called the *Third Eye*[1] and the *Splenic Center*[2] .

Opening the Third Eye and Splenic Centers

1. Begin by warming up the *Heart* chakra by rubbing in a circular motion and visulizing a green flower opening. Next, activate the *Throat* chakra by tapping it and visualizing it opening up like a blue flower. You can also use the energy of your dominant hand (fingers together pointing in towards the throat) by slowly

---

[1] The Third Eye is the color purple, and a reflection of the Water-Sign *Cancer*.

[2] The splenic Center is the color of bright orange, and a reflection of the Earth-Sign *Capricorn*.

Current Order	Revised Order	
Taurus	Aries	
Aries	Taurus	*Current*
Pisces	Virgo	*Spiritual*
		Age
Aquarius	Capricorn	
Capricorn	Leo	
Sagittarius	Gemini	
Scorpio	Libra	
Libra	Aquarius	
Virgo	Sagittarius	
Leo	Cancer	
Cancer	Scorpio	
Gemini	Pisces	

Figure 13.2: Revised Order of the Ages

opening this center with an opening motion of the fingers[3]. Feel the energy in your finger tips open the throat center.

2. Next, open the *Upper Solar Plexus* using the same process, visualizing a pink or dark yellow flower. Feel the *Upper Solar Plexus* as an empty vessel waiting to be filled by the energy from the *Throat* chakra. Both the *Throat* and *Upper Solar Plexus* may begin to feel warm with varying degrees of elation.

3. Next, use the same process to open the *Mouth* chakra (visualizing an indigo flower, a very dark bluish purple), and the *Lower Solar Plexus*, visualizing a bright yellow flower. This should cause a feeling of warmth from your throat, extending all the way down to the lower solar plexus.

4. Next, use the same process to open the *Third Eye* chakra, visualizing a purple flower, and the *Splenic* chakra, visualizing a bright orange flower, located between the *Lower Solar plexus*, and *Pubic* chakra.

---

[3] Fingers together pointing towards the throat center, slowly spread the finger tips away from each other in a widening circle.

Chapter 14

The Twelve Faces of God:
Physical Bodies

Life After Death

I believe that everyone, at some point in their lives, wonders about the "After Life". Whether there is one or not—and if there is—what is it like? The following Chapters will make you an expert in this esoteric field.

The diagram in *Figure 14.1*, is composed of information very carefully garnered in this lifetime. It is not simply a repeat of the same old system left over from many centuries ago. As such, be aware that it is an entirely different system based upon entirely different criteria. I mention this to prepare you for the possible shock that this information might bring, not corresponding to what you have previously learned and perhaps, even teach.

If you recall, Jesus had trouble teaching the New Message for the New Age, just two thousand years ago. And although modern metaphysical teachers are not physically crucified, there is a great tendency to write them off as "nutters" which, sadly, turns a difficult task into an improbable one.

The New Metaphysics

The old *Seven Chakra System*, while still valid, was released into the general population, expressly for the 2000 year period just finishing. By the same token, now, the *Twelve Chakra System* is being released into the general population expressly for the next 2000 year period, known as the *Orange Age*.

The Time Travelers philosophy in no way looks upon the earlier works with disdain and in fact incorporates the earlier work as a fundamental basis on which to build. Although this method of incorporating new methodology and substance over the old, it is a natural re-occurrence, progressing from Age to Age. Each Age brings with it new and appropriate information, and people to disseminate it. However, many may feel put upon, having to learn something new. While I sympathize with these people, metaphysical progress must evolve to be current for the tasks at hand, which will be demanded from us as the higher vibrations and configurations, impinge upon our delicate nervous systems. To avoid the subsequent pain that accompanies major changes, such as moving from one Age to another, it is more than incumbent upon metaphysical leaders and teachers to be the first to learn the *New Metaphysics* so that they may integrate it with their knowledge of the *Old Metaphysics.*

In addition to helping you come into a measure of Cosmic Consciousness, a thorough study of the individual component bodies that make up the composite human being will greatly increase and promote understanding of how the human complex works, and thus bring the healing arts one step closer to replacing the pharmaceutical gridlock in which medical practice now exists. It is to this end that I share the following observations.

At a certain level of Cosmic Consciousness, the Human body is perceived as consisting of twelve separate bodies which work together to form the thirteenth. These bodies are divided into three groups of four. The densest group of four is the Physical group.

The diagram in *Figure 14.1* represents the various chakras as found in a man. Note the ascending scale of color going from lower vibratory colors at the lower body, and progressing up to the highest colors at the head. I have included the names of each body as well as its associative planet.

Physical Bodies

The physical body is composed of three separate bodies, each superimposed and existing within the same relative space, separated only by degrees of vibration. There is, of course, the outer physical shell or "Meat" body, that you are most familiar with. As your densest body, this "vehicle" interfaces with the Third Dimension, and allows you to move and have experience in the outer world. It is a hard shell that protects you from the outside, and has a relationship to your Soul, the way your car has a relationship with you.

In *Figure 14.2*, we see the various chakras involved with each of the physical bodies.

Note in the diagram, the *Pubic* center is the color *red*, denoting a male. This center in a female is the color *burgundy*. This is why, interestingly enough, that although called the 12 chakra system, we only count 11 chakras in either a man or a woman.

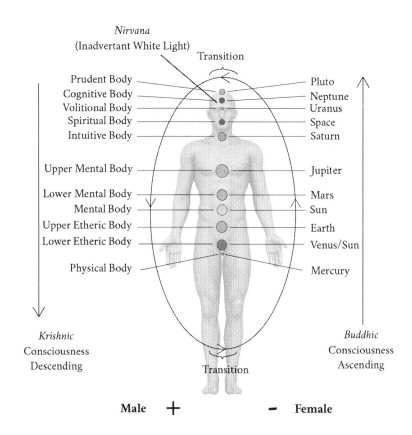

Figure 14.1: Wheel of Consciousness

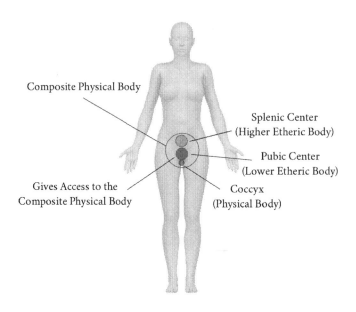

Composite Physical Body

Splenic Center
(Higher Etheric Body)

Pubic Center
(Lower Etheric Body)

Gives Access to the
Composite Physical Body

Coccyx
(Physical Body)

Figure 14.2: The Physical Bodies

The Physical body by itself has no personality or motivation other than to eat and sleep. If you have ever visited an Elderly Care Home, you may have seen cases of extremely elderly people who fit this description. These are cases of the astral bodies dying before the physical body. In some cases, the elderly unwittingly become psychic vampires, sucking the energy from all those around them in order to stay alive. You will know when you have encountered one, because you will feel drained from the experience. When in the presence of this type of being, unless you do not mind giving them some of your energy, you can protect yourself by holding your hands together, and if you are seated, cross your legs and fold your arms. You may find yourself doing this instinctively. If you are feeling generous, hold their hands in yours, or give them a hug.

The Lower Etheric Body

Existing inside of your densest Physical Body, there are two more physical bodies. They walk around with you when you walk around. You may think you do not know about them, but you do. The next densest body to your Physical Body is your *Sexual* Body. In Germany it is called the *Doppelganger* or Double. Here it is called the *Etheric*

Double or the *Lower Etheric Body.* It is the vibratory center of the Physical Body, and it contains your personality, and is primarily concerned with procreation. In sexually active people, this center has a great deal to do with their activities. Singles Bars or singles chat rooms on the Internet attract this body. It is usually very interested in the physical attributes of the opposite sex. Hollywood has capitalized on the sexual charisma of great personalities.

As we mature, we become more in tune with our higher vibratory bodies. The hormone levels that control our sexual activity lessen and allow us to discover the more discreet portions of our minds and spirit. People who feel they have died sexually have developed a form of apathy in this body. Also people who have a flat and uninteresting personality may suffer from an underdeveloped or damaged sexual body.

The Higher Etheric Body

Next is the last of the three, the *Higher Etheric Body* or *Electrical Body.* It processes the life force that enables you to be alive and healthy. It charges up at night when you are asleep, by raising about six inches above your physical body.

If you have ever gotten overly tired, and started to doze off, you might have experienced the unpleasant sensation of suddenly jumping awake, as though there was a loud noise or explosion? This was your Higher Etheric Body prematurely exiting to replenish the life force before you were completely asleep. This startles your denser bodies that would normally be asleep which in turn causes your Higher Etheric Body to "crash" back into you, jarring you awake.

You may have also experienced a state of paralysis, where no matter how hard you tried, you could not move. This also might have been accompanied by the sound of rushing wind, or in the most severe cases, a series of explosions that might resemble a seizure. This is the beginning of what is called an Etheric Projection. The next time this happens, calm yourself, and let the experience happen.

Earth-Bound Souls

Upon the death of the physical body, what has been referred to as an *Earth bound Soul* is usually just the wanderings of discarded Etheric Bodies, but in some cases, it is an earth bound Soul. As the Soul withdraws from the physical plane, the Lower Etheric body—because it is no longer connected to the Higher Etheric body—will usually die within days after the death of the physical body. This is the body that people usually "see", immediately after a loved one dies.

If the Soul is relatively unevolved, or unusually interested in the sexual activities of others, then its interest through the lower Etheric body can become a problem. It is the combination of the Lower and Higher Etheric bodies that produce what we call Ghosts[1].

Health Issues

The health of the Higher Etheric body is extremely important to the general health and vitality of your entire being. It was mistakenly thought to be the sexual body, in women, by eastern mystics, because when it shut down, it also shut down the sex drive, and when it was activated by a Healer, it occasionally resulted in spontaneous orgasm. It is located between the navel and the sexual center, and is associated with the spleen. For this reason it is sometimes called the *Splenic Center.*

Unfortunately, most women who work in the business place with men shut this center down as a professional courtesy. This forms a sort of psychic chastity belt and can cause premature sexual shutdown and general health problems by promoting less hormonal activity. Indications of this problem, other than the obvious, are the appearance of many vertical lines on the upper lip of females. The Higher Etheric body—as with the Sexual body—can with safe and simple meditative techniques, and non invasive energy manipulation, be brought back to health.

Review of the More Important Points:

1. The Physical Body is made up of three separate bodies.

2. Each body occupies the same physical space, but each vibrates at very different rate of vibration.

3. Although the three bodies work in tandem to function as the "Physical Body", they can be separated and can operate independently[2].

---

[1] This combination of Etheric bodies can last for many years, even though they long been discarded by the Soul.

[2] Upon the death of the outer physical shell, which usually, dies first, it is the combination of the Lower and Higher Etheric bodies that make ghosts.

4. The densest body forms the outer "meat" shell. It is our work horse. It interfaces with the external three dimensional universe.

5. The next less dense body is the *Sexual* or *Lower Etheric body* that contains a portion of the indwelling *Self* in the form of the Personality, which is the outer expression of the Ego.

6. The last of the three physical bodies is the least dense, and the highest in vibration. It is the *Electric* or *Higher Etheric body*. It is this body that is responsible for processing the life force (orange energy) that animates the Physical Body.

This concludes Chapter 14. The next Chapter will examine some additional information on the Physical bodies.

CHAPTER 15

THE TWELVE FACES OF GOD:
PHYSICAL BODIES (CONT.)

All of the *Physical* Bodies we have looked at—as well as the *Mental* and *Emotional* bodies we will be studying in subsequent Chapters— are related to a specific part of the spectrum as a color and are also related to either the Sun or a Planet within our Solar System and a particular Sign of the Zodiac.

I believe this knowledge was perfectly understood by the Ancients, which represents the "parent" system for all subsequent astrological systems, but which has been very watered down and refined over the Ages into the form you see today, losing most of its original importance as relates to a method for unlocking the secrets our true nature. I believe the work done by these ancient metaphysical giants to be extremely valuable, and it is with this in mind that I have revived the original knowledge and share it with you as I believe it was originally meant to be understood.

Before you became involved in "time" and the "physical universe", you shared your Soul with your other half. Upon entering the plane of duality, the two of you were separated. There is an intense desire in both of you to reunite. Although you and your mate, as male and female, have the same number of centers (chakras) within your physical bodies, the emphasis, due to polarities, are different. In this lesson we will look at some of these differences.

The diagram in *Figure 15.1* is not meant to be an exact representation of the human aura. It is, instead, meant to emphasize the basic differences, in the purest sense, between a man and a woman. Remember that what is shown below is the preference for the pure man and the pure woman, and not meant to represent an ideal. In actuality, there are any number of combinations including the exact reversal of the preferences shown. The vertical order remains the same, only the horizontal order can be exchanged.

In *Figure 15.2* we can see how the differences between a man and a woman originate. The white globe at the top represents pure potential in the primordial 2nd dimension (Christ principle) before its decent

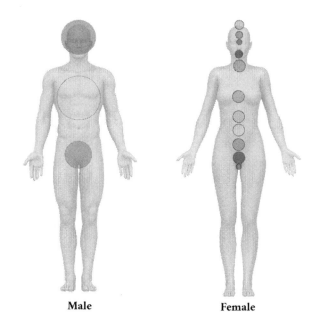

Male   **Female**

Figure 15.1: Basic Differences Between Men and Women

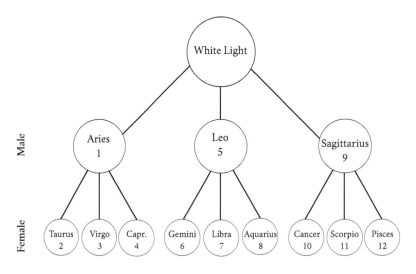

Figure 15.2: Origin of the Basic Differences Between Men and Women

into the planes of duality. Notice that it sub-divides into a trinity consisting of red, yellow and indigo globes. This combination represents the male principle. Below this are further sub-divisions representing the female principle. In our current discussion we are focusing on the physical portion of the male trinity (the red globe, Aries), and its component sub-divisions—brown, burgundy and orange globes as *Taurus*, *Virgo* and *Capricorn* respectively.

Another way to look at the chart is to consider the white globe as our Sun. The trinity—consisting of the three Fire Signs—represent the three component principles of the Sun, namely; *outward expansion* represented by *Aries*, *inward collapsation* represented by *Sagittarius*, and the *static state* represented by *Leo*. This leaves the nine remaining Signs which represent the nine planets, starting with *Taurus* whose planet is *Mercury*, and ending with *Pisces* whose planet is *Pluto*.

I realize this is somewhat different than what is currently thought, but please understand that these designations only serve to place each of these Signs—as *vibratory* principles—into their proper position in relation to the Sun, and are not dependent upon there being any planets at all. The astrological systems currently in vogue are based upon *magnetic* influences and positions of heavenly bodies upon the earth, and subsequently upon you. The system we are studying is based upon the *vibrational* sub-structure of the Solar System as a macrocosmic pattern found also in human beings as a microcosmic sub-structure, and has nothing to do with magnetic influence or position of the planets.

We learned in the last Chapter that the physical body can be separated into three components. This can be thought of as actually four separate bodies. The three separate component bodies and the forth which is the non-separated composite body that functions as a totality. It is this composite body functioning as a totality that we will look at first.

The Composite Physical Body

The composite physical body, as with all of the bodies we will study, can be identified with a color in the spectrum. The color for the composite physical body is usually thought of as being bright red, although it actually extends from infrared up through the visible range of red.

The Sign of the zodiac with which the composite physical body is identified is the Sign of *Aries* the Ram. Aries, a Fire Sign represents the *outward expansion* of energy from the Sun, and is the abstract representation of the lower vibratory range of physical form. It also manifests as male sexual energy.

According to Time Travelers tenets, Aries—as a Fire Sign—is associated with the Sun, and not the Planet Mars, as is held in modern Astrology. Aries is also associated with the shell of vibrating energy that extends out from the Sun, and encompasses the three inner planets, Mercury, Venus, and Earth. As was mentioned before, the system we are presently learning has nothing to do with Astrology, or Astrological influences, so please do not let the differences confuse you. They are two completely different systems, founded upon an entirely different basis. Only the names of the Signs, and their general characteristics are the same.

Although both males and females have a composite physical body, there are some differences. The *composite* physical body is considered more as the *male* polarization in relation to the three *component* bodies, which are considered as the *female* polarization. *Aries* as a center (chakra) is the *Male Sexual Center*. The male view point tends to identify more with the composite body than with the separate component bodies comprising it. Emotionally *red* is identified with rage, on one end of the red spectrum and courage on the other, and is responsible for the saying "seeing red". Red is also the color seen in the aura near the area of an injury. In the art of energy manipulation, red is a principle healing color.

The three component bodies would have to have been considered by the Ancients as the female polarization, as opposed to the composite body, which, as we said above, is considered male. It is important to note that the *component* body known as the Sexual Body—although both males and females have one—is known as the *Female Sexual Center* (burgundy). This is because the male sexual center resides in the composite body (red) rather than in the central component body where the female sexual center resides. As was mentioned in the last Chapter, this polarization within the sexual centers is the reason we count only 11 chakras instead of 12.

To restate this, a man's sexual center radiates *red* energy directly as *Aries*, The Ram while a woman radiates *burgundy* from her sexual center as Virgo, The Virgin.

The Physical Body

The first of the three component bodies comprising the composite physical, is the Physical "Meat" Body. Here we can actually see the physical differences in polarization between male and female. This body, whether it is male or female, is identified with the Earth Sign, *Taurus* The Bull and is related to the *Coccyx Center* at the base of the spine. Its color is associated with the vibratory part of the visible spectrum that is dark red or brown.

Taurus represents the first kingdom—the Mineral Kingdom—and is related to the vibrating shell of energy encircling the Sun that extends out to just beyond the vicinity of the planet Mercury, the planet with which it is associated.

The Sexual Body

The next component body we learn about is the *Sexual* Body or *Lower Etheric*. Although both males and females have one, it is considered as the *Female Sexual Center*. It is identified with a spectral color that is burgundy, or a sort of dark grayish or blackish red to dark purplish red or reddish brown. This color in the human aura, indicates feelings of lasciviousness.

The diagram in *Figure 15.3* represents the various colors associated with the human aura. The major difference between a man and a woman is that the *Sexual Center* is *red* in the man, and *burgundy* in the woman.

The Sign of the zodiac associated with this center is the Earth Sign, *Virgo*. It is vibrationally connected with the shell of energy encircling the Sun, that extends out to just beyond the vicinity of the planet Venus, the planet with which this body is aptly associated, and represents the second kingdom—the Plant or Vegetable Kingdom. It is this body that is used in what is called bilocation, the ability to be in two places at the same time. The practitioner can instantaneously transport his sexual body to any distance. Once there, he can by an effort of will, lower the vibrations of this body so that it may be seen, and even interacted with. This was brought to an art, by a few Yogi Adepts from the far East.

The Electric Body

The last physical body we will look at is the *Electric Body* or *Higher Etheric*, sometimes called *Astral Body*. This too is considered a female

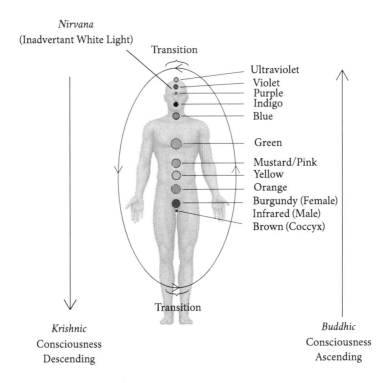

Figure 15.3: The Colors of Associated with the Human Aura

polarity, and is associated with the Earth Sign, *Capricorn*, the Goat. Its spectral color is orange. An orange color when observed in the human aura denotes different kinds of pride, depending upon the shade. The darker shades indicate hurt pride. The lighter orange indicates pride of ownership or accomplishment. A proud father will exhibit a very bright orange. This is the color of the life force or vital energy and because it is connected to the Insect Kingdom, has a great deal to do with the nature to organize and socialize.

The higher etheric is associated with the vibrating shell of energy encircling the Sun, that extends out to just beyond the vicinity of the planet Earth, the planet with which this body is associated, and represents the third kingdom—the Insect Kingdom[1].

Empathic ability relies upon being able to detach this body, and overlay, or merge it with another's, while the practioner remains awake, for the purpose of healing. The most advanced Empaths use both the lower etheric body, which remains in the physical body, and the higher etheric which overlays upon another persons lower etheric body. This ability can be learned, and is indispensable for those of us who are involved in the Healing Arts. You can tell if you are empathically inclined by whether you can feel another's illness.

For example, if you are around someone who has trouble breathing, do you suddenly feel as though you are having trouble breathing? You may have been told that you have a big imagination or that you are a hypochondriac. The truth is that you are probably a budding empath. This faculty was little known in the present time period and so, tragically, was either discouraged or ignored in children.

This concludes Chapter 15. In the next Chapter we will continue with our study of the Twelve Bodies by looking at the four Mental Bodies.

---

[1] As a note of interest, because of orange energy and its role as the life-force necessary to produce sentience, this would indicate a presence of physical life-forms exclusively on the third planet from the Sun. This could very well be a part of our Suns *signature* that it sends out to other Solar Systems, encoded in its radiant energy we call light.

Chapter 16

The Twelve Faces of God: Mental Bodies

Residing within and above the physical—in terms of vibration—is the *Mental Body* which deals with planning and abstract thinking. Like the Physical Body, it is also made up of three separate bodies, the first of which is the *Lower Mental Body* or *Lower Mind*. This is the beginning of what is called the *Mental Plane*. Here we are concerned with the facts and figures of the world. It is a lightning fast computer. Although this body is associated with the Animal kingdom, it is highly evolved in Man. Idiot Savants and child geniuses exhibit some of the amazing abilities available in a sufficiently developed Lower Mental Body.

The next higher body in vibration is the *Higher Mental Body*. This is the mental body that the majority of Mankind is striving to master. Here we are learning how to apply judgment and powers of discrimination. The better Generals throughout world history had a highly developed Higher Mental Body. This faculty is usually exceptionally developed in Time Travelers, which gives us the ability to understand the many subterfuges so prevalent in politics and business of the time.

This was an Age where the Masters of deceit flourished and the ability to lie and deceive was greatly rewarded with power and wealth. The general population was not able to discriminate and therefore were fair game to the more crafty predators among them. Unfortunately, some Time Travelers—because of their highly developed powers of discrimination—will become caught up in this process as predators, which would produce internal conflict within their highly developed spiritual and moral bodies.

The highest vibrational Mental Body is the *Intuitive Body*. This faculty gives the user the ability to "know" without knowing. In the present time period, advanced Man was beginning to learn to use this Body.

Review of the More Important Points:

1. The Mental Body resides upon the various Mental planes of existence, and is concerned with the mental abilities and qualities

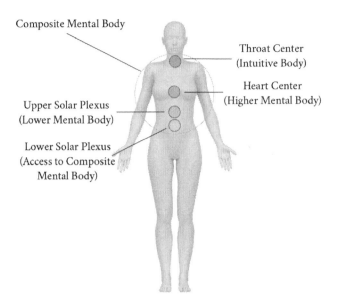

Figure 16.1: The Mental Bodies

of the mind.

2. It is composed of three separate bodies.

3. Each body occupies the same physical space, but each vibrates at very different rate of vibration.

4. Although the three bodies work in tandem to function as the Mental body, they can be separated and can operate independently.

5. The lowest in vibration is the *Lower Mental Body*. It is like a calculator. It resides on the lowest mental plane.

6. The second part of the Mental Body is the *Higher Mental Body*. It is the central part that contains a portion of the indwelling "Self" in the form of the Ego.

7. The last mental body is the *Intuitive Body*. It has the highest vibration. It bestows the faculty of intuition or knowing without knowing. Very few people of today had developed this faculty to any degree. Numbering among those who have are many Psychics, Mystics and of course, Time Travelers.

Each of the mental bodies we have just learned about is related harmonically to a specific part of the spectrum as a color and is also related to either the Sun or a Planet within our Solar system and a sign of the Zodiac.

Although on the inner planes the Mental Body appears to reside in simply a higher vibratory level from the physical, it actually has a multidimensional placement that is in the center of our being. As was stated earlier, the mental body is a composite of three separate mental bodies. It is associated with the Fire Sign *Leo* the Lion. Its polarization is male and represents the *Male Heart Center*. Although it extends—in the human body—from above the throat to below the solar plexus, it is accessed through the lower portion of the solar plexus. It is here we find a kind of animal courage or aggression[1].

The Composite Mental Body

The Composite Mental Body is bright yellow in color yellow and in the context of mentality, is associated with pure intellect. It represents the abstract mind. Leo is also associated, as the central vibratory reflection of the Sun with the shell of vibrating energy that encompasses the three central planets Mars, Jupiter, and Saturn. Leo, a Fire sign, represents the central consciousness of the Sun and houses that indwelling portion of the self known as the *Super Ego*.

The Lower Mental Body

The Mental Body is made up of three component bodies, the first of which is the *Lower Mental Body*. This body is the color of dark yellow (Male, mental) or pink (Female, emotion). It is this pink color that is responsible for the saying "sees through rose colored glasses". This pink vibration causes its practitioner to live in a fairy land of wonderfulness, a hard reality to maintain in today's world. Marilyn Monroe is an example of a pink Gemini. A certain shade of pink is associated with the feelings of puppy dog love. The dark yellow is sometimes connected with the "little professor" aspect of the personality. This is where you find the "know it all".

The *Lower Mental Body* is associated with the Air Sign, Gemini the twins. In terms of birds, this air sign it is most akin to the hawk[2].

---

[1] This can be thought of as the "fight" response of the "fight or flight" syndrome.

[2] Some Geminis look like birds of prey, with pronounced hawk like features.

The vibratory shell for the Lower mental Body extends out from the Sun to the vicinity of the planet Mars. Physically, it is accessed through the upper half of the Solar Plexus, and represents the upper echelon of the fourth kingdom—the Animal kingdom. Domestic animals usually have this center well developed. It is here we get feelings of right and wrong. It is also where we get a "gut" feeling about things. It is in this area of the Solar Plexus that we feel the numbing fear that is the opposite of courageousness, and this is the reason the term "yellow" is associated with cowardliness[3].

Because of our close connection with the Animal Kingdom, and the wide spread abuse and killing of animals all over the world, we are affected through sympathetic vibrations in this body, causing us to have unwarranted feelings of fear in some of the more sensitive of us. This is also the body where the feelings of shame are experienced.

The Higher Mental Body

Next is the *Higher Mental Body*. This body is composed of all shades of green, the most central point of all of the colors. This is the *Female Heart Center* and is associated with the Air Sign *Libra* the Scales. Libra as an air sign is akin to the owl. Many Male Libra's of this type will actually look like a bit like an owl.

Libra represents the center, or balance point of the spectrum. Its planetary connection is the vibrating shell of energy that extends out from the Sun to the vicinity of the planet Jupiter, the fifth and most central planet out of the nine and represents the fifth kingdom—the Human Kingdom. Whereas Virgo housed the personality and Leo houses the *Super Ego*, Libra houses the *Ego*. It is rigidly centered in its green habitat. On the negative side is where all manner of selfishness originates. In addition, it is the home of procrastination and is responsible for the saying "can't get off of the dime". It is also responsible for the saying "green with envy".

The darker the shade of green the more intensely selfish. As we move through the darker shades we find such old favorites as greed and vanity, not to mention avarice. It is no accident that our paper money is green. The lighter the shade, the more philanthropic, and in the central shades we find tranquility. There is a certain emotional openness in the lighter shades of green within the Female Heart Cen-

---

[3] This can be thought of as the "flight" response of the "fight or flight" syndrome.

ter that prompts the saying "wears her heart on her sleeve". In the extremely light shades we find superficiality and frivolousness. Since this is the balance point, it gives the Human Being an extra view point over the animal kingdom.

The animal has only four view points, which results in *emotionally* based decisions. "This or that", "black or white". The Human Kingdom has five view points. It is this extra view point that allows a detached reference point that gives the ability to discriminate or discern. This results in *intellectually* based decisions, and is one of the primary differences between animal and human behavior.

One of the problems with this body—for the inept—is the inability to make a decision. Because of the capability of seeing all sides of a decision as being equal, it becomes difficult to make any decisions at all. This type of person does not like to argue because they can understand and sympathize with both sides equally. Certain types of mental illness derives from the negative aspects of this body in the form of procrastination in combination with fear found in the upper solar plexus, usually experienced as a gone feeling. Agoraphobia[4] and other kinds of phobias in this category can produce a paralysis of fear. Color therapy and energy manipulation can greatly diminish—if not completely cure—these types of phobias.

In men, the sign of Libra makes for excellent Generals, as an example, General Eisenhower was a Libran.

The Intuitive Body

The last Mental Body is the *Intuitive Body*. This body has as its vibrational color base all shades of blue and is accessed through the throat center. It is associated with the Air Sign *Aquarius*, the Water Bearer. Many people think that it is a water sign because of this but it is actually the highest vibrational Air Sign. It is here the saying "feeling blue" comes from. The darker the shades of blue, the more serious the mood. This can produce feelings of melancholia. The lighter the shades of blue, feelings of spiritual devotion can be experienced. The highest shades of blue denote the highest feelings of altruism, inspiration, and selflessness. This can be a problem for the practitioner because they can easily be victimized and taken advantage of.

The planetary connection for the Intuitive Body is the vibrating

---

[4] Fear of open spaces.

shell of energy that extends out from the Sun to the vicinity of the planet Saturn and represents the sixth kingdom—the Super Human Kingdom. This, being an air sign, is most like the eagle.

Aloofness or cold loftiness can be a problem for this body. Feelings of sympathy emanating from the Intuitional body at the throat center is responsible for the saying that one is "choked up". Also, fear emanating from the upper solar plexus can sometimes cause this center to shut down which is why we may have difficulty speaking when we are scared.

The lightest blue type of Aquarian can also vie with the pink Gemini for the title of "air head". The lighter shades produce a feeling in those around them of trust-worthiness and good-naturedness.

The addition of intuition to the Human Being gives him six separate view points. This distinction is the difference between the Human Being and the Super Human Being that is coming into being in this time period. A difference as great as that between the human and the domesticated animal.

This concludes Chapter 16. In the next Chapter we will look at the four emotional/spiritual bodies.

CHAPTER 17

THE TWELVE FACES OF GOD: EMOTIONAL/SPIRITUAL BODIES

In terms of vibration, the Spiritual Body resides within the same space and above the Mental Plane. It is also a composite body in that it is made up of three separate bodies. This body represents Male Emotions and Female Spirituality which is extremely interesting in that this body vibrates in resonance with the color indigo. Indigo, when viewed clairvoyantly, looks almost black and for all practical purposes is a virtual void. What this means is that fundamentally men exist in an emotional void and women exist in a spiritual void.

Before you react to what was just stated, let it be known that this is a good thing and will be quickly explained as such. As you progress in this Course you will begin to understand that true emotions and spirituality are born out of the blackness of the void. Since the blackness of the void is much too severe for us as Human Beings to tolerate, indigo is nature's way of imitating the void without actually having to use it. The result to us is the same. The dark indigo spiritual body by itself is a terrible experience for us. It is so dark that we can experience nothing except that we do not want to be there. It is necessary for us to experience nothingness in order to cause us to let go completely. This is a major and absolutely necessary developmental component at the highest level of Human evolution.

The Spiritual body is comprised of three component bodies, the first of which is the *Volitional Body*. This is a center of will-power and focus. Some of the greatest leaders throughout history had developed this faculty. In the Male polarization, it is the "Eye of the Tiger" sought by the combatant. It is used to pierce the veil of mystery sought after by mystics. However, it is sometimes a veil of tears for women.

At certain levels of vibration, the volitional body can emotionally be a place of deep suicidal depression for the uninitiated. If you can see colors around people (Auras), this depressed condition appears like a dark purple band around the eyes, giving the bizarre feeling that you are looking at a masked bandit or a raccoon. This condition can be quickly alleviated by color therapy and energy manipulation.

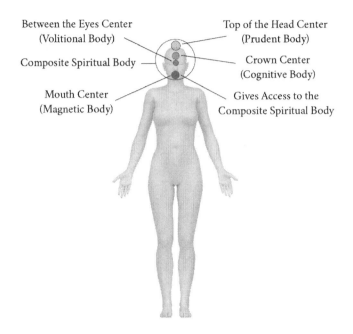

Figure 17.1: The Emotional/ Spiritual Bodies

Here is something you can try if you feel depressed. Meditate upon or gaze at a bright orange object or light. This will lighten up your aura and provide a measure of immediate relief.

Remember that men can be susceptible to the emotional effects of the Volitional Body, just as much as women can use it for focus and will power to become top athletes. The Volitional Body is currently very underdeveloped in most of the world population.

The next higher vibrational vehicle is the *Spiritual Cognitive Body*. It is the place where spiritual knowledge is known. It conveys to the user great wisdom and clairvoyant powers. It is the central part or heart of the Spiritual Body and contains a portion of the indwelling "Self" in the form of the discrete Super Ego. Our greatest profits and spiritual teachers had access to this faculty. Emotionally, this body expresses spiritual power. Taken to extremes, it can produce megalomania or what is know as a God complex.

The highest vibrational Spiritual Body and the last in line is the *Guardian* or *Prudent Body*. This body interfaces with the spiritual or Fourth Dimensional "outside", just the way our physical outer shell interfaces with the Third Dimensional "outside". It filters out unnecessary or unwanted spiritual influences.

It also is a regulatory body in that it moderates the amount of spiritual energy flowing into the lower vibrational vehicles, which regulates the amount of inspiration a person may have. If you are uninspired, this body may be asleep or perhaps has become damaged through psychic attack or drug abuse.

It can be awakened by direct energy manipulation. Sometimes this body, for some reason (many times drug related), goes into overwhelm and begins to produce an inordinate amount of fear. This in turn shuts down the spiritual flow through the system. In severe cases, this can result in a form of severe paranoia, agoraphobia, or even violent behavior. This is especially true of long term cocaine, or heroin users and short term crystalline methamphetamine (crystal meth) users. Sometimes a single trip on lysergic acid will cause this body to go into permanent shut down.

Review of the More Important Points:

1. The Spiritual Body is made up of three separate bodies.

2. Each body occupies the same physical space but each vibrates at very different rate of vibration.

3. Although the three bodies work in tandem to function as the Spiritual Body, they can be separated and can operate independently.

4. The first and lowest vibrational vehicle is the *Volitional body*. It functions as a lens for focus and will power but can have a negative emotional influence.

5. The next less dense body is the *Spiritual cognitive body*, that contains a portion of the indwelling "Self" in the form of the Discrete Super Ego which is an expression of the Soul. It gives access to universal knowledge.

6. The last of the three bodies is the least dense and the highest in vibration. It is the *Prudent Body*. It spiritually protects the lower bodies and also controls the flow of spiritual energy, including its complete shutdown!.

Each of the spiritual bodies we have just learned about is related to a specific part of the spectrum as a color and is also related to either the

Sun or a planet within our Solar system and a sign of the Zodiac. As was stated earlier, the spiritual body is a composite of three spiritual bodies. It is associated with the Fire Sign Sagittarius, the Archer. Its polarization is Female in relation to the Fire Sign, Aries[1].

At this point, a distinction needs to be made as to the actual male-female relationship between the three Fire Signs, Aries, Leo, and Sagittarius. All three fire signs are male in relation to their component signs, however among the Fire Signs Aries has a polarization that is male in relation to Sagittarius, which is female. They are in every way equal and opposite. However, Sagittarius is still male in relation to its component signs Cancer, Scorpio, and Pisces. Leo is a composite of, and the center of, the combination of Aries and Sagittarius. In other words Aries, which is positive, represents the Father as a polarized male. Sagittarius, which is negative, represents the Mother as a polarized female. (Polarized, in these cases, means they are each one half of a composite whole). Leo on the other hand is a Universal Positive, in that although it is male, it is formed from the balance of both male and female, born out of Aries and Sagittarius, which becomes the center as the Universal Child, or Son... (Sun), or Daughter... (Planetary system). Aries represents the third dimension in its every aspect. Sagittarius represents the fourth dimension, and Leo represents the Fifth dimension.

Sagittarius is the Male Spiritual Center and the Female Emotional Center. Although it extends, in the human body from the top of the throat to the top of the head, it is identified with the mouth center. Its color is indigo, a very dark purple. It represents abstract emotionality for men, and objective emotionality for women. Sagittarius, a Fire sign, represents the Sun at night, or the returning energy of Aries. It is the force that holds all of the planets in their orbits.

Sagittarians have tremendous magnetic powers that are many times not noticed by those around them. They are catalysts that cause people and things to come together. Sagittarius's planetary connection is the vibrating shell of energy that encompasses Uranus, Neptune, and Pluto. Sagittarius reflects the dual function of the mouth, in that it produces great orators, and singers, as well as great gourmets. For those of you that can see Auras, look for indigo around the mouth, especially

---

[1] Leo, a composite of Aries and Sagittarius, represents the Sun—although male—is not polarized with the other two Fire Signs but is instead polarized with the nine remaining Signs, which represent the nine planets.

those with Sagittarius rising. People who run indigo energy through their hands, have what looks like dirty hands to the clairvoyant. This is not a negative, but strange when you first notice it. They, along with people who run orange energy, can be very hard on machinery, especially cars.

The Spiritual/Emotional Body is made up of three component bodies the first of which is the *Volitional body*, a center of creative, will and emotional power, and is located at the Between the Eyes Center, and is also called the Third Eye. This center is associated with the Pineal Gland. The pineal gland is a small organ attached by a stalk to the posterior wall of the third ventricle of the brain. This is towards the back and above the cerebellum. It is called the pineal gland because it is shaped like a small pine cone.

The Volitional body has the spectral vibration of the color purple. It is associated with the Water Sign, Cancer the Crab. Its planetary connection is the vibrating shell of energy in the vicinity of Uranus. (Cancer is physically connected to the nose, and relies upon the olfactory senses.)

The next Spiritual Center is the *Spiritual Cognitive Body*. It is located at the Crown Center (or the Thousand Petaled Lotus). It is associated with the Water Sign Scorpio. Its planetary connection is the vibrating shell of energy that extends out from the Sun to the vicinity of Neptune. Its color is violet. It is also associated with the billions of cells that comprise physical brain, which in this connection, is a facsimile of our Galaxy, the Milky Way, with its billions of stars. Scorpio is associated with the eyes. You may have heard the expression, "Scorpio eyes". It is very distinctive and once you have identified it, will be able to spot them easily. Scorpio is physically connected to the eyes, and relies upon sight.

The Crown Center may seem like an unlikely place for Scorpio, which is usually associated with the sexual center. However, Scorpio has gotten a bad rap. It is the only triple sign in the Zodiac. Traditionally the Eagle, the Snake, and the Scorpion. In the system we are learning, Scorpio also has three centers. First is its own center, the Crown Center, this is the well spring of great emotional and spiritual power. which is the Male spiritual center. Next is the Female Heart Center, under Libra, a place of great intellectual capacity, and thirdly, is the Female Sexual Center, under Virgo, sometimes called the "Little King", in men. It becomes apparent that Scorpio is very involved with

Christ Consciousness, in that these centers represent three out of four of the manifestations of Christ. Only Leo is missing.

It is unfortunate that many Scorpio's are fascinated with the least virtuous part of their nature.

The last center is the *Prudent Body*. It is associated with the Water Sign Pisces. Its color is ultra violet or gray. Ultra violet is the highest spiritual vibratory color within a human being. Gray is the spiritual color of fear. This aspect of fear is very interesting in Pisces. This is not the usual animal fear we are most familiar with, that emerges from the solar plexus, it is, instead, the kind of fear we call dread, or mortal fear, or the sometimes paralyzing fear of the unknown. Fear is the regulatory device that the Prudent Body uses to control all of the rest of the bodies. In this sense, the Prudent Body is a combination of all of the rest of the bodies. Although this is a place from which great wisdom and diplomacy is born. It can be said that this body is the "Jack of all trades", but master of none.

The center for Prudent Body is at the very top and center of the head, and is, (oddly enough), called the Top of the Head Center. Its planetary connection is the vibrating shell of energy in the vicinity of the planet Pluto. This center is usually associated with the pituitary gland.

Review

A good way to start this review, is to look at what we have covered, from the other way around. First have the solar system, which when viewed from a distance could be considered a ball of expanding white light. This stage in consciousness is the present goal of Humanity.

If we separate white light into its three primary components, we find a combination of infrared, yellow, and indigo. Infrared, (red) under the sun sign Aries, is further broken down into the three earth signs, Taurus, Virgo, and Capricorn. Their colors, respectively, are brown, burgundy, and orange. Primrose yellow, under the sun sign Leo, can be separated into the three air signs, Gemini, Libra, and Aquarius. Their colors, respectively, are dark yellow (sometimes pink), all shades of green, and all shades of blue. Indigo, under the sun sign Sagittarius, can be divided into the three water signs, Cancer, Scorpio, and Pisces. Their colors, in turn, are purple, violet, and ultra violet (gray).

Notice that this is a linear system. What is meant by this is, the signs line up according to the spectrum, in a linear fashion starting with the lowest vibrational earth sign, and winding up with the highest vibrational water sign. We begin with the lowest vibrational fire sign, Aries (red), which rules the lower male torso, and corresponds to the energy (Kundalini) found at the male sexual center. In this case, at the coccyx center at the base of the spine, and not necessarily at the male pubic center.

The next step is the break down of Aries into its three components, the first of which is Taurus, (brown) found at the anal center. Next is Virgo, (burgundy) found at the female sexual center. The third and last component of Aries is Capricorn, (orange) found at the Splenic center, a point between the sexual center and the navel. Next is Leo, (bright yellow) located at the solar plexus. Abstractly, Leo is also considered the male heart, and rules the middle section of the male torso. Specifically Leo is found through the lower portion of the solar plexus. Leo when separated into its three components, produces Gemini, (dark yellow or pink). These are known as the twins. which occupies the upper portion of the solar plexus.

Next is Libra (all shades of green) at the heart center. Libra is also considered the female heart. And thirdly is Aquarius, (all shades of blue) located at the throat center. After Aquarius, we find Sagittarius (indigo, a very dark blue purple) at the mouth center. Broken down into its three components, we first find the Water Sign Cancer, (purple) located at the spot between the eyebrows. Next we find Scorpio (violet) located at the crown center. Last in line, is Pisces, an ultra violet, which looks like a light lilac or gray. Clairvoyantly, gray is usually identified as the color of fear. Pisces is located at the top of the head, and is the only sign to have direct access to this center.

Note that physically, in each group of three, each Sun Sign comes first, followed by its three component signs.

Chapter 18

Detailed Examination of Consciousness:
Christ Consciousness

What is the difference between God, Christ, Cosmic, Buddhic and Krishnic consciousness? By examining the evolution of consciousness from the primordial pre-manifestated state to present, I believe we can find a simplified understanding of what is otherwise a complicated and difficult subject fraught with a morass of varied interpretation and emotional bias.

The definitions contained in this Chapter and those that follow in this series supersede all other definitions contained in the Course. By this I mean if a contradiction occurs in the definitions found in earlier Chapters and those now being presented, defer to these later definitions. This is because a more exacting examination of consciousness produces a more exact definition and hopefully a more precise understanding of the underlying mystery of the nature and structure of consciousness.

Consider our earlier examination of primordial consciousness when we saw that the void contained a substance[1] with the potential for life, which was capable of producing all that we experience today. We further saw that this substance was subject to continuous inherent vibration which produced polar opposites.

At one pole (negative pole) was the primal void, which was the Ether devoid of all motion or vibration. At the other pole was the void experiencing maximum motion or vibration of the Ether which produced "white light" as a natural consequence. Remember that these poles exist in the same space, separated in time by the relative time it takes vibration to go from maximum to minimum and back again in a perpetual "sine wave".

The nature of vibration dictates that there is a stair step process of ascending vibration from the void to white light and descending vibra-

---

[1] Ether—an all-pervading, infinitely elastic, mass-less medium formerly postulated as the medium of propagation of electromagnetic waves. The void, or that which fills the void. Einstein's "fabric of space".

tion back again to the void. Each of these four states[2] is the beginning of a different kind of consciousness, i.e.: Cosmic consciousness, Christ consciousness, Buddhic consciousness and Krishnic consciousness respectively. Together, these form something called *God consciousness* which is a grand gestalt beyond these individual kinds of consciousness. In other words, God consciousness exists in a way so unified as a whole that its properties cannot be derived from a simple summation of its parts.

The void is the birthplace of what—according to Time Travelers tenets—is called the *Sagittarius principle* which in its most extended state is called *Cosmic consciousness.*

The white light state is the birthplace of what—according to Time Travelers tenets—is called the *Leo principle*, which is the beginning of *Christ consciousness.*

The action of going from white light towards the void is part of the nature of what we, again according to TT tenets, call the *Aries Principle.*

Ascending vibration[3] upon the Ether is—according to TT tenets—called the *Buddhic Principle* while descending vibration[4] upon the Ether is called the *Krishnic Principle*[5].

The diagram in *Figure 18.1* shows the various components of Christ consciousness in terms of the colors of the spectrum and the Signs of the zodiac.

Note that the white ball symbolizes Christ Consciousness and although the subdivisions are shown as being parts of it, these subdivisions are the property of Cosmic Consciousness (which includes the void) as a polar opposite to Christ Consciousness. God Consciousness in its simplest form is the simultaneous awareness of everything shown on the chart, including the void.

The white light state shown is static in that it is without motion. We have seen this state before as the goal of Buddhic consciousness. In that context it is called *Nirvana.* It is also thought of by many as highest "Heaven" in the western world and by many others as God. What is found here—as emotional content—is called bliss or ecstasy

---

[2] The void, white light, moving from the void to white light, and from white light to the void.

[3] From the void to the white light state.

[4] Coming from the white light state to the void.

[5] Note that the Buddhic Principle is part of the nature of the Sagittarius Principle, and that the Krishnic Principle is part of the nature of the Aries Principle.

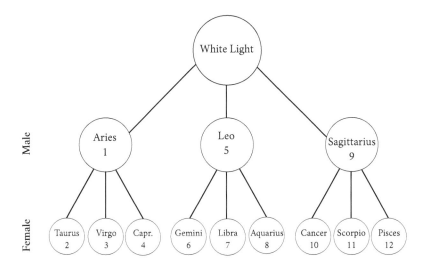

Figure 18.1: Christ Consciousness

when compared to any other state of being.

It is interesting to note that Christ consciousness in this primal state does not exhibit that which we term "love", so predominately associated with this consciousness. This ability or quality which is so characteristic of Christ consciousness, does not appear until we experience it in its subdivided descent into duality. This is simply because of the necessity of reflected selves, not possible until the planes of duality. It is important to note that Christ Consciousness, at this master level, is composed of all other components of manifestation and potential kinds consciousness including all component levels of what is exclusively considered as various sub-levels of Christ consciousness. The two exceptions that cannot be included as sub-divisions of Christ consciousness are Cosmic consciousness, which is a polar opposite of Christ consciousness, and God consciousness, which contains both Cosmic and Christ consciousness as integral parts of itself.

We have stated that all other kinds consciousness—with those exceptions stated above—are derived from Christ consciousness as sub-components. It is for this reason that many think that the "Christ" is in fact God. We can understand why many would also believe in this state-of-being as the ultimate goal for humanity.

It should be pointed out that Christ consciousness, within human beings, exhibits motion as an *outward* expansion from a fixed centralized position, which impinges upon others as love. Cosmic consciousness on the other hand exhibits motion as an *inward* contraction from a fixed position that is the opposite of centralized which manifests as enlightenment and bliss.

It is important to understand that those who seek God consciousness have chosen a much more difficult course of action than those who seek to simply "return to the Christ" and must have as a prerequisite already progressed through the lessons of Christ consciousness. This is not to deride the latter, for Christ consciousness is a critical, vital and necessary choice to each and everyone of us in our spiritual progression. However please note that as I understand it many Christians believe the direction of creative intent of Christ consciousness is "returning to the Father" through Christ, to reside in "Heaven". On the other hand, the direction of creative intent of God consciousness, from all indications, is one of manifestation into the Third dimension as "Heaven on Earth". This would suggest that those who simply seek refuge in the Christ will at some time feel the urge to re-descend into matter as a necessary continuation of spiritual evolution.

I feel that the above spiritual dichotomy is at the heart of much unnecessary spiritual confusion and subsequent lack of unity. For this reason I believe that it is obviously prudent in order to help to alleviate this confusion for us to endeavor by all available means to understand the structure of consciousness and its rules of engagement.

CHAPTER 19

DETAILED EXAMINATION OF CONSCIOUSNESS: COSMIC CONSCIOUSNESS

Cosmic Consciousness, what is it and how is it different from other consciousness? It has been stated that Christ consciousness is all-inclusive. Everything we know about our universe could be said to be contained within the Christ Principle. So where does Cosmic consciousness reside? It resides *outside* of Christ consciousness as a polar opposite.

This may sound strange or even impossible when you first read it but never the less it is true. Perhaps if we take a moment to compare Cosmic and Christ consciousness in relation to God consciousness, we can clear up any confusion.

Essentially, we are studying something called God consciousness and its constituent parts. If we subdivide God consciousness into its most basic parts we find two components called Christ consciousness and Cosmic consciousness. These two components are diametrically opposed. By this I mean they are *exactly equal and opposite*.

Christ consciousness as a principle occupies everything that is *internal* to God consciousness, and its method of motion is one of *outward expansion* while Cosmic consciousness as a principle occupies everything that is external to Christ consciousness and its method of motion is one of *inward expansion* or *contraction*. We will get into more detail as we progress. For now, understand that there is a trinity composed of God consciousness and its two principle components.

We can recognize from the Christian idea of the trinity, the "Father" principle of the trinity as God consciousness. We can also recognize the "Son" principle of the trinity as Christ consciousness. This leaves Cosmic consciousness as the "Holy Ghost" principle.

On a more personal level, we can see the Christ principle existing as what one considers as oneself or personality, or the insouling something that differentiates each of us from all others. Conversely, we can see the principle of Cosmic consciousness existing as all that is not considered the self. It is the cohesive something that exists beyond the individual as a principle of collectivity that holds everything together.

We learned in the last Chapter that the primordial positive pole is also the primordial Christ. We also learned that this same place is called Nirvana by some and Highest Heaven by others. That these seemingly different places are in fact the *same* place is an astoundingly important piece of information and one I believe most metaphysical researchers have missed.

I personally believe that Christ consciousness is but an interim step to God consciousness and to attempt to make it otherwise, as an end in itself, no matter how tempting or expedient this may seem, is to deform the children of God. It is with this in mind that the TT tenets will endeavor to sort out the more confusing aspects of consciousness in the hope that future researchers may build upon it.

Remember that there are two major paths. One is the Angelic path with Heaven and existence within the Christ as the goal. The other is the God path with a continuing participation in creation, and never ending unfoldment of God consciousness as the goal. Of the two, Heaven is obviously a much easier closed ended goal through the regimented Angelic hierarchy and is relatively easily attained. God consciousness on the other hand is open-ended. It is a never ending accumulation of knowledge, power and space, and in addition to this, *all* that the Christ principle confers as well. God consciousness being all-inclusive includes all that the Christ is without being confined by it. As we recall, the Christ principle is all that is internal in God consciousness, and can be thought of as the personality, or (quality) of God or if you will, the "heart" of God. Cosmic consciousness in contradistinction is all that is external. God consciousness contains—but is not limited to—these two components of all that is internal and all that is external as well.

It is good to remember that the basic difference between God consciousness and Christ consciousness is one of placement and perspective. While God consciousness contains, in perfect balance, both Christ and Cosmic consciousnesses, with the Christ as the internalized sum and quality of the Self, in Christ consciousness God exists as an externalized parent.

Detailed Examination of Consciousness:
Buddhic Consciousness

We saw in the last two Chapters that vibration acting upon what is called the "Ether" or Einstein's "fabric of space" causes a polarization which is a condition of opposites. One pole is pure energy without vibration or motion. The other pole is the same pure energy in a state of maximum vibration or excitation. Because the negative pole—the void—appears to be first in order, it is called the First dimension. According to Time Travelers text, this is called the *Prime Reality* or *First Reality*.

The other pole, because of its relationship to the First pole becomes a second place or dimension which is contained by the first. Because of this duality we call it the Second dimension or *Second Reality*.

Please note that the Second dimension is *contained* by the First dimension. This means that the Primordial 2nd dimension as a polar opposite is contained in the center or inside of the Primordial 1st dimension.

If you will examine this place with me you will see that the primordial 2D is a place of endless white light without any distinguishing features. Although we have identified it as the primordial Christ, it is static and without the expected feelings of love that one associates with Christ consciousness. This is because it is completely self-contained and exists in a pure state of "Self" without any concept of something outside of itself. The lack of reflected replicated selves removes the characteristic magnetic attraction and interaction that would normally identify this as a place or property of what is loosely termed the Christ.

The 2D, upon closer examination, is everything we identify as Nirvana (Seventh Heaven) and the apex of Buddhic consciousness. While this may seem strange and paradoxical at first, it is completely understandable given the fact that *all* facets of consciousness and created form are derived from the same primordial substance. The myriad differences that arrive from this cosmic womb are all simply unique combinations of the original. Knowing this takes much of the mystery out of the equation, but after all this is what we are attempting to accomplish isn't it?

The above brings up an interesting point. If the Primordial 2D as a place or state of being is the primordial Christ, then how could it also be Nirvana or Buddhic consciousness? Does this mean that they are the same?

They are in a sense the same, but in a larger and fundamentally more important sense, they are completely different. It is this difference that we need to examine. Stated as simply as possible, Christ consciousness exhibits a condition of permanence when achieved as a result of the *accumulation* and *centralization* of consciousness within an evolving human being while at the same time achieving an inherent state of detachment from the separate constituent parts and levels of this consciousness. In other words, Christ consciousness is a completeness beyond the accumulated parts, but is always experienced from an enclosed position as the internal self. Given the above definition, even the personality could be considered a (albeit greatly removed) part of Christ consciousness.

When we contrast the above with Buddhic consciousness, we find we are dealing with the same place and the same nature of consciousness, but from the *outside*. Furthermore and most importantly, Buddhic consciousness is achieved through detachment but not accumulation of the separate constituent parts and levels of consciousness. This means that while Christ consciousness is total and complete as regards the various levels and kinds of consciousness that comprise it, Buddhic consciousness can be defined as a sort of stair-step climbing on top of each component part or level through a process of acquisition and subsequent rejection, and then only in an upward or higher direction in vibration. It is this upward motion that distinguishes it from all other forms of consciousness. This has prompted the argument that the goal of Buddhism seems to be annihilation rather than enlightenment. This is understandable considering the traditional Buddhists goal of total rejection of the 3D through successively lesser incarnations until the need to reincarnate is completely transcended. (Devolving, finally to the level of an insect! The idea of devolvement is not widely accepted in the west because of a natural repugnance to this idea by the western mind.)

In the mechanics of Buddhic consciousness, a point is reach where there is a sudden realization of white light or "enlightenment". According to Time Traveler text, this is called "inadvertent" white light.

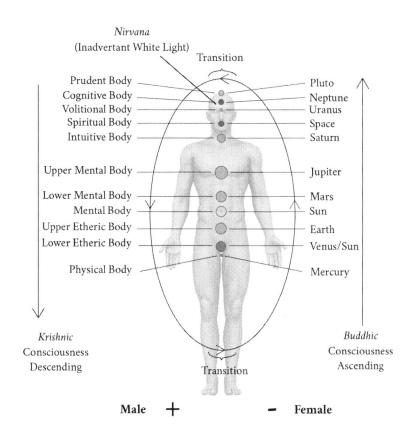

Figure 20.1: The Wheel of Consciousness

Inadvertent because of the upward motion through the structure of consciousness (a result of consecutive detachment) within a human being and as a consequence of being subjected to a state of simulated nonexistence so devastating that it forces a simultaneous and inadvertently cohesive realization of the separate constituent parts and levels of consciousness, which results in a temporary experiencing of a state of white light, and greatly expanded state of consciousness called "enlightenment". What this means is by detaching from each successively higher vibration, a place is reach where we run out of vibrational environment. It is here we hit the "void", called the *Waveless* state.

Because total detachment always results in a sudden realization of white light, there is a resultant white light state that comes into realization at this time. This achievement is *temporary* because of the upward motion that has been brought into being by the very methods used to achieve it. It is this temporariness and non-centralized consciousness (bliss rather than love) that is characteristic of the "enlightenment" stage of Buddhic consciousness. It is here, in enlightenment, that we begin our descent into denser and lower vibratory levels of consciousness, who are called "Buddhas of Compassion", because they forego this exulted state of Being in order to help those of us who are "less fortunate". Although a nice sentiment, according to Time Traveler doctrines this is simply the other side of the "wheel", and the beginning of what is called *Krishnic consciousness*. In other words, the practitioner has no choice at this point but to descend. Built into the illusion is the belief of wanting to descend in order to help those less fortunate.

CHAPTER 21

DETAILED EXAMINATION OF CONSCIOUSNESS: KRISHNIC CONSCIOUSNESS

Krishnic consciousness was so named after its chief practitioner Lord Krishna best known to us from the Bhagavad-Gita. This part of consciousness represents the return from white light to the material planes or 3D.

Technically, Krishnic consciousness is said to be representative of Vishnu the preserver which represents both birth and death. Originally Vishnu represented the complete wheel of life and death which would include Buddhic consciousness as one half of the wheel. When I refer to Krishnic consciousness however, I am referring only to the descending masculine side of the wheel[1].

The major distinguishing characteristic of Krishnic consciousness is that of a continual selfless giving regardless of consequence. The practitioner finds himself descending from an exalted level of consciousness to lower levels of consciousness to help those less fortunate then himself. Unfortunately, there is an inadvertent reduction of vibration resulting in the practitioner arriving with the same level of consciousness as those he would help. We humorously call this the "Law of Punishment for the Good Samaritan".

According to Time Traveler definitions, we can identify Krishnic consciousness as a coming from the light and moving towards lower vibrations of the physical planes through a systematic reduction in vibration. This identifies it as belonging to the Aries principle—the universal male principle. We know that Aries is the outward expansion of consciousness from the light (or Sun) to the void. This includes all outward motion.

Krishnic consciousness is identified with the number 9 and as a power structure. This is in contradistinction to Buddhic consciousness which is identified with the number 7th. To understand why these numbers are significant, we need to see that in Buddhic consciousness we can only reach the 7th dimension, and then only temporarily. It is almost impossible for one to follow the process in consciousness

---

[1] The Buddhists refer to this consciousness as *Buddhas of Compassion*.

while going from Buddhic consciousness to Krishnic consciousness. I believe this is why there is so much confusion about it in these two religions.

Basically, what happens is when one reaches enlightenment, they automatically inherit the 8th and 9th dimensional structures as well, as part of the 10D. This is not seen by the practitioner because of a certain degree of "snow blindness" due to the sudden and persistent advent of white light. While experiencing all of this, and its attendant levels of ecstasy, there is little thought of investigation. The turn around point then becomes the 9th dimension which is a power structure and is naturally positioned to radiate downward in vibration into the physical planes.

In God consciousness the 9D is used to radiate power into the 3rd dimension, but without the degeneration of consciousness found in Krishnic consciousness. The power is radiated from a permanent and fixed position. This would be so for Krishnic consciousness as well but unfortunately, whether we call the practitioner Krishnic or Buddhic, the result is the same. Because of the flywheel effect of forward motion there is a turning around, for the insouling consciousness, from going into ever higher levels of vibration, to going into ever lower levels of vibration, hence the "wheel". This is one of the greatest mysteries of this time period.

The reason advanced seers and clairvoyants could not understand the true meaning of this phenomenon is because of overwhelming feelings of compassion and an irresistible desire to return to help those less fortunate souls. This was understood as *Dharma*[2] in Hinduism. The difficulty they faced was in understanding exactly what the duty should be and understanding exactly how far one had to go before violating the universal laws of balance.

The Buddhists describe "Buddhas of compassion" as Great Souls who could have gone on to a permanent state of bliss, but forgo this in order to help humanity. I tell you that this is absolutely not the case. They cannot continue on. No one ever has, and no one ever will. At least not by the methods used.

To better understand the role each type of consciousness plays in our reality, think of all consciousness as being part of the universal 3D. The 3D forms a trinity. In any trinity are three distinct positions;

---

[2] The need to do one's duty regardless of personal feelings.

These positions are summed up below:

1. There is basic form or outer shells that function as vehicles, which we see as the physical body in the physical trinity.

2. The indwelling consciousness which we consider as ourselves and which we see as the personality in the physical trinity.

3. And last is the power structure, which we see as the ability to accomplish and have motion in the physical trinity.

In terms of consciousness, we can identify number one above with Buddhic consciousness. We can identify number two above with Christ consciousness, and number three with Krishnic consciousness.

Krishnic consciousness, as a polarization in relation to its twin sister Buddhic consciousness, is male. If you will recall, there are three major principles in creation regarding vibration and motion. We have labeled these: outward motion or the Aries Principle (Krishnic consciousness), inward motion or the Sagittarius Principle (Buddhic consciousness) and stationary centralization or the Leo Principle (Christ consciousness). Because of the continuous cycle or wheel effect, Buddhic and Krishnic consciousness are forever consigned to exchange with one another.

In summary, we need to make a basic distinction within the Aries Principle. We have seen that there is outward motion of energy into lesser levels of vibration until a vibration-less state is reached, and also that there is an outward motion from the source that maintains its levels of vibration as white light. As regards Krishnic consciousness, we see that it falls into the first category. The second category, as an extension of continuous radiance and power, is part of what I call God consciousness. Escape from the Buddhic/Krishnic wheel is achieved by coming into a centered position upon the wheel which incorporates both directions and consciousness. This centering is called Christ consciousness whose fundamental motion is one of expansion rather than movement via levels of vibration.

CHAPTER 22

DETAILED EXAMINATION OF CONSCIOUSNESS: GOD CONSCIOUSNESS

As has been stated previously in *A Course in Time Travel*, our goal is the never-ending pursuit of God consciousness. It is never-ending because there is no end to the possibilities and levels of Being that can be experienced.

Mystics who have experienced a taste of what is available have all been at a loss to even begin to express what happened to them. These "little touches" are so far beyond our everyday mundane experience that it is impossible to communicate into words and indeed in anything less than the experience itself. We are reduced to terms like "ineffable" and "consummate" when trying to verbalize what we have experienced or what we believe these mystics to have experienced. It would be like trying to tell a blind person what the starry night looked like or trying to communicate to a child the delights of adulthood.

As we have said previously, God consciousness is a perfectly balanced array of all other consciousness and viewpoints. This basic combined viewpoint—once achieved—can be enhanced as to quality, ability and understanding. This means that one can attain God consciousness and appear very flat and uninteresting in the beginning levels.

How is God Consciousness Different from its Components?

In our examination of the various kinds of consciousness the final one in the series is God consciousness. We will take a look at why God consciousness is superior to any other kind of consciousness and summarize its distinguishing features.

As we have seen in the last few Chapters, there are four major components of God consciousness, namely: Christ, Cosmic, Krishnic and Buddhic. We have seen how each is an integral part of God consciousness and how each differed from the other. Although we have seen many indications of what God consciousness is, in this Chapter we will gather together those qualities and definitions into one place for purposes of reference and further understanding.

In God consciousness, we see an interplay of all of these consciousness as being inseparable. This interplay and fusion of consciousness into a single entity that gestalts far beyond its individual components, is probably the most distinguishing feature of God consciousness. We have previously defined God consciousness as having the universal qualities of:

1. Omniscience—Having total knowledge; knowing everything.

2. Omnipresence—Present everywhere simultaneously.

3. Omnipotence—Having unlimited or universal power, authority, or force; all-powerful.

However, for the individual the above qualities exist as potential that can never fully be reached. The reason for this is in the definition of the unlimited potential for us as individual beings in our pursuit of God consciousness.

In simpler terms, one of the most wonderful things about coming into God consciousness is the fact that we are finite beings expanding into unlimited potential. It seems then that we, as finite beings, need a more specific set of definitions then has previously been given.

Specific Definitions for God Consciousness
(As Pertains to Human Beings)

1. Unattainable.

2. As having unlimited levels of realization.

3. At the same time, expanding and contracting, rather than simply expanding as in Christ consciousness or contracting as in Cosmic consciousness.

4. As being an on going process rather than something one attains all at once. An ongoing process without end.

This means that no two persons who attain God consciousness will probably be at the exact same level of understanding and mastery at the same time[1]. It also means that probably no two persons will process God consciousness at the same rates of realization. There is an upper

---

[1] Encouraged differences and variety in consciousness continues to be a central theme even in God consciousness.

limit as to the absolute rate of realization, which is termed *instanta-neous*. In an unlimited and infinite medium, expansion/contraction[2] from a single point such as occurs within the consciousness of an individual, *instantaneous* becomes finite and measurable. If my understanding is correct, this state of instantaneousness is a natural part of the 13D.

How can a person come into the process of being *God conscious* and still function in the "real world"? As we approach the Thirteenth dimension—which I have glimpsed and believe to be a most perfect state of existence—anything less than God consciousness would prohibit one from existing in this long sought after "Heaven on Earth". They seem to go hand in hand.

I have stressed in *Observing the Paradoxes* maximizing your 3D experience by being all that you can be from moment to moment while at the same time staying detached from the results. Consider that coming into a state of God consciousness should greatly enhance your 3D experience rather than cascading it into an untenable situation. In fact, if you believe yourself to have attained levels of God consciousness and are experiencing dark realities and reactions to your efforts, then obviously you have deluded yourself into believing something that is not true by definition.

Remember that your Time Traveling Oversoul has its own agenda. High on it's list of priorities is manifesting through you in a state of God consciousness and that of achieving the 13D.

This concludes our series on the various types of Consciousness. It was in no way meant to be exhaustive but rather as a reference and guideline for the lay person interested in pursuing multidimensional consciousness.

In the next Chapter we will begin a series of meditation techniques called the *Fifth Dimensional Meditations* which signal the halfway point in our studies. Up until this point we have examined some ideas and theories about consciousness and discussed the reasons why I believe they are true. Now we will begin a series of practical techniques developed for achieving what we have studied and discussed thus far.

---

[2] As a convenient measure, I have referred to this as expanding (out/in) at the speed of light, however this in no way is meant to limit the definition of unlimited.

CHAPTER 23

FIFTH DIMENSIONAL MEDITATION: EXERCISE ONE

Our physical perceptions are confined to our five senses. Some of us have developed a sixth sense which we call *intuition*. Our sense of sight allows us to see into the third dimension. Our senses of hearing, smell, feeling and taste all allow us to better perceive different vibratory levels of the third dimension. Notice that none of these senses give us access to any place other than the 3D. As we develop our sense of intuition, we begin to sense there may be other possible dimensions other than just the third dimension in which we seem to live.

Because all of our senses are outward-facing we are greatly aware of the outside, which is the 3D panorama so evident all about us. Gradually as we mature spiritually, we become aware of an inner consciousness that is somehow observing life through us. We become curious about this "inner consciousness", hence the questions: Who am I? Where do I come from? Where am I going? Why is all of this happening? How is it possible for all of this to happen? Did I exist before? What happens when I die? Where was I before? Who or what was I? Is there a creator? Am I that? How can I know more? Do more? Be more?

These are a few of the questions that have plagued mankind from the beginning of our existence. We have studied and explored and prayed and meditated until there is nothing left to study, explore, pray and meditate about. We have enumerated, postulated and theorized until there is nothing left to enumerate, postulate and theorize about, and yet nothing ever really changes for us spiritually. We have seeming change as we progress through each Age, but this is like praying for warmer temperatures when it is cold in the winter and thinking that our prayers were answered when spring and summer comes.

We have seen that the 3D—from our viewpoint—is outward-facing and that the 4D, as a mirror image universe of the 3D, is inward-facing. We also find we cannot—as a unified viewpoint—easily observe both universes at the same time.

The meditations that follow in this and the next fiew Chapters are designed to solve this monumental problem. It has been stated in this Course that the fifth dimension is composed of the third and fourth dimensions combined. We will now learn how—through meditation techniques—to develop a viewpoint that is truly 5D. We have already looked at a few of these techniques in earlier Chapters as a prelude to this section.

I believe we can assume that you are still stuck in the 3D. You may think you are not. This is part of the power of 3D illusion. Before we can take the first step on the road to 5D mastery, we need to be willing to let go, on some level, of all that we are and all that we know. Because this is not a simple task to contemplate intellectually, we will do it in a form of meditation.

Assume with me for the moment that you are stuck in the 3D. Eventhough you have material wealth and you are the great so and so of the world, and you know all and can fly around the room at will and many fall down on their knees in your presence, let me say that you have to let go of all of this in order to go on. I appeal to that part of you that knows you are in a cul-de-sac of ego. Your ego will fight very hard to convince you that what is being said here is all nonsense and a waste of time. You cannot really blame it for not wanting to be dethroned. Our ego can be like a wanton child. It cares not about adult concerns and wants only what it thinks it wants at the moment. It is however necessary in the continuum of existence of each individual to evolve to a point where the ego is willing to forgo some of its immediate pleasures in favor of a continuing spiritual development.

1. First, it is important to realize there is the possibility of experiencing *much* more than what you are experiencing now.

2. Next is the understanding and utilization of the tools that are being provided to you in order to realize these possibilities.

3. Next is the desire to give these suggestions a valid try.

4. Finally is actually doing what is suggested on a consistent daily basis with as little resistance as possible, in the belief that necessary and positive changes are truly taking place in your internal world and consequently, are inevitably changing your external world as well.

Once you are able to observe these suggestions you are ready for the first step.

There is an overwhelming tendency for us to fall back to sleep, dreaming that we are accomplishing all that we wish to accomplish, in terms of expanding our consciousness. Without a terrific desire to awaken, it will be next to impossible for you to do so. Others of us are simply too busy answering the demands of daily 3D life to incorporate these techniques on a daily basis. It is always easier to fall back into old patterns that work for us rather than take the time and concentration it takes to incorporate new patterns, eventhough the new patterns might point to eventual enlightenment and liberation.

What we will accomplish in the first step isa shift from the 3D view point to the 5D view point. This means going from the familiar forward progression of time and events to a combination of *inward* and *outward* simultaneously.

Meditation

A very important point to be aware of is that acquiring the Fifth Dimension also means *expanding in size* in terms of our internal viewpoint and consciousness. We are about the size of a ping-pong ball or smaller. This means we can only experience a single chakra at a time as we travel within our being due to the limitations of our size. Without a degree of mastery, which the normal person usually does not have, it is difficult if not impossible to travel at will from one center to the next. In the completed fifth dimensional viewpoint, we are expanded to a size larger than our physical body. This allows us to experience all of the previously separate centers simultaneously.

There is a physical center within your physical body that is the point where the third and fourth dimensions meet and pass through each other. It is the point in the center of the chest where you find an indentation. Its color is green. Within the color green we are looking for the most central shade. In our meditation it helps to have a physical location and a color to visualize. It is also associated with middle C, for a sound reference.

There is a natural point of existence within you where you are balanced at your very center. This means you are viewing the outside from the very center of yourself. This place is the physical place mentioned above at the center of the chest.

We cannot see all of the higher vibrational centers contained in the 4D environment because they reside behind—or within us—in vibration. We could, by facing inward, see the 4D centers, but this would not help accomplish our goal of achieving a 5D viewpoint. This meditation technique is to help us identify where the starting point is. If we can identify with our heart center at the sternum, and the color green, this should help us find the correct placement.

This portion of the Chapter will be devoted to the beginning level of *Fifth Dimensional Meditation* techniques. We will start by concentrating on opening and warming up the *Heart center* located in the middle of the chest at the sternum, and not the actual area where the physical heart is located. Feel for the indentation located between the breasts.

We need to learn and practice these beginning techniques on a daily basis to prepare us for the more advanced *Fifth Dimensional Meditations* later on, which are absolutely necessary to progress in this course. It shouldn't take more than five minutes a day to soon become proficient.

A centering process has to take place to bring you into the heart center. This can be accomplished through stimulation of the heart center by rubbing it in a circular motion with the finger tips of one of your hands[1]. Do this until you can feel some heat begin to generate there. It might also help to visualize a middle, to light green flower that is opening[2].

Our goal is to maintain an open heart center on a permanent basis whether we are in meditation or not. Something to look for is the warm feeling in your heart center that will be with you from now on. Use this warm feeling when you relate to others. It is called *love*.

---

[1] I use a counterclockwise motion, but you might find clockwise better for you.

[2] With practice this center can feel quite warm if not hot. If you do not feel warmth right away, this is OK. It will come with time.

Chapter 24

Fifth Dimensional Meditation:
Exercise Two

As we progress in our meditation, we need to heal up some of the third and fourth dimensional damage that has accumulated at the various centers. We always begin our meditation at the heart center because it centers us and allows a balanced expansion. In most people, the heart center is full of pain and disappointments. It is the center of relationships. It is through this center we share our love with others.

When we experience pain through broken relationships or death of loved ones, this center has a tendency to shut down rather than go through the natural grieving process that keeps it healthy. When this center shuts down it locks the pain away as though in a feeling-proof vault by freezing time. The end result is that this person no longer is able to love or participate fully in any relationship. The reason people allow this center to shut down is for the obvious reason of not wanting to feel the pain. There is an inordinate fear of opening this center and having to unfreeze those moments that have been waiting all of this time to be felt. The pain felt there was never as bad as it was thought to be, and usually dissipated in a matter of seconds. Sometimes there was grieving but it only lasted a short time, soon to be replaced by the joy of being able to feel love again.

Working on Another Person

After gaining verbal permission to open the heart center, I first open my heart center by energizing my right hand and pointing my fingers into the area of the sternum at the center of my chest. I make an opening motion by slowly widening my fingers. As this center opens I can feel warmth begin to radiate out from it. I switch hands, holding open my heart center with my left hand, and with my right hand I repeat the procedure with the person I am working on. It is not necessary to physically touch them. I make a note of how my heart center feels and compare it to the way it feels when I open the other person's heart center. Usually I feel varying degrees of pain ranging from a mild sting to pain that has put me on the floor. Typically I feel something wedged into the center of their heart center. It is like frozen energy that varies in size from a tooth pick to an icicle. It is usually either clear in color or black.

I know that whatever I am feeling they are feeling at the same time. I will verbally confirm this by describing what I feel and see. Next I will ask permission to remove the frozen energy. I have never had anyone say no, although some were reluctant. Next I will, with my right hand, take a hold of the tip of the frozen energy with my finger tips and slowly pull it out of the heart center[1]. I would also concentrate on feeling and seeing the object and the pain moving out of both my heart center and theirs at the same time[2].

Once the object was externalized I would feel the absence of pain in my heart center and know that the same thing happened for them. I would dispose of the frozen energy by flinging it down towards the ground and seeing it vaporize in a white flash in mid air. Next I would generate feelings of love in my heart center and transfer it to their heart center. I would intensify this by radiating loving energy from the palm of my right hand in close proximity to their heart center. I would confirm and explain each thing as it transpired, and make sure that they understood and confirmed it back to me. I would stay in touch with them for a couple of days by phone and Empathically. I would tell them that there might be some grieving, but this was a good thing and not to worry.

In order to go to the next level of meditation, we need to clear our heart centers. We can do this by using the procedures above, only upon ourselves. I would suggest stimulating your heart center everyday. I have literaly worn holes in a couple of my t-shirts doing this.

This concludes this Chapter. In the next Chapter we will examine in detail the techniques and results of opening up the throat and top of the Solar Plexus centers.

---

[1] While watching the procedure, other clairvoyants have described what the object looked like as I pulled it out, which usually matched my earlier description.

[2] Remember that I duplicated their pain in my heart center.

CHAPTER 25

FIFTH DIMENSIONAL MEDITATION:
EXERCISE THREE

In the last Chapter, we examined some techniques for opening and clearing the *Heart Center*. In this Chapter, we are going to learn how to open the *Throat Center* and *Upper Solar Plexus Center*.

Our primary goal—as our Time Traveling Oversoul—is to come here to the third dimension from outside of time and to be able to manifest here in full consciousness in accordance with the intent of the Universal Mind. Along the way we will discover simple previously unavailable remedial techniques that can be used by everyone right away. Some of these techniques might easily overcome seemly unapproachable human conditions. From time to time I will point out some of these remedies as and where they occur in each Chapter.

The *Throat Center* and *Top of the Solar Plexus Center* are polar opposites. In a normally operating person, the Throat Center is dominant. This produces a nice blissful feeling of wellbeing in the Solar Plexus area. In people who are fearful, angry, or anxious, the Solar Plexus Centers have become dominant, which produces fear, anger, and anxiety. This is why people who suffer from this problem have difficulty speaking when they are afraid. They become choked up with emotion. Acid Reflux is a physical symptom of this condition. When they are angry, they find themselves saying things that they would never normally say, often causing irreparable damage to relationships with friends, co-workers and loved ones. If this anger is channeled down to the lower centers, then physical violence might occur. The pharmaceutical companies are getting rich producing chemicals to mask this out of balance condition. The obvious remedy then is to re-establish the proper relationship between these two centers.

Additional Meditation Technique

1. Start the meditation by placing your dominant hand over your Heart Center at the center of your chest[1]. Rest it there firmly

---

[1] Your Heart Chakra is not found at the actual heart area. It is instead located at the indentation at the center of your chest at the sternum and extends out to about the

until you feel warmth being generated. Visualize a green flower opening.

2. Next, place your other hand over the top of your Solar Plexus until you can feel some warmth there.

3. Next, with your dominant hand gently tap your Throat Center, located just below the Adams apple. This is to wake it up.

4. Next, make an opening gesture with your finger tips at the Throat Center. As you slowly widen your fingers, feel the increase of energy there. Visualize your throat center as a blue flower opening up.

5. Next, switch hands and while holding your Throat Center open, make an opening gesture with your finger tips at your Upper Solar Plexus, located just above the navel and visualize your Upper Solar Plexus as a gold (men) or pink (women) flower opening up. Also look for nice tingling feelings in both your throat center and the top of you solar plexus.

Continue this until any feelings of fear, anger, or anxiety have subsided. If you have a lot of fear or anger or anxiety, you might want to repeat the meditation whenever you can through out the day until the feelings subside and are replaced by feelings of well being.

This may sound silly, but it helps to talk to your Solar Plexus. This is where your "inner child" lives. If you have chronic anxiety, then this would be a good technique to cultivate. While rubbing your Upper Solar Plexus, say something like this: "I am here now and everything is alright. You don't have to worry, I am in charge now and I will take care of everything". Feel that part of you relaxing in trust. Another variation of this is to pat your Solar Plexus and say over and over, "You are a good boy (girl), I am here now, everything is alright". This should greatly reduce the level of anxiety or fear.

This concludes this Chapter. In the next Chapter we will examine in detail the techniques and results of opening up the Mouth and Bottom of the Solar Plexus centers.

---

size of a ping-pong ball in the average person.

Chapter 26

Fifth Dimensional Meditation: Exercise Four

The *Mouth Center*, which is Indigo in color, is a window to Sagittarius and represents abstract[1] power and spirituality. Its counterpart, located at the *Lower Solar Plexus*, is a window to Leo (Bright yellow) as raw courage and abstract intellect[2]. Courage, without a sense of spirituality, can degenerate into foolhardy or destructive behavior and even rage, and therefore spirituality must lead. On the other hand, spirituality without the courage to take action leads to physical inaction.

To balance these two centers is to expand the fifth dimensional heart center from the Mouth to the Lower Solar Plexus.

In the meditation that follows and all of the 5D meditations thereafter, we need to do something called *observing the paradoxes*. What this means is that we need to learn to do two things at the same time during meditation. Namely, *exertion* and *relaxation*.

First a little background for why this is necessary and why the meditation is designed in this way. Our primary concern is how to achieve the first levels of Cosmic consciousness found in the Sixth dimension while at the same time maintaining a basic level of Christ consciousness found in the Fifth dimension.

As was mentioned in an earlier Chapter, the difficulty of progressing through the 5D on our way to the 6D is getting trapped inside of Christ consciousness. There is a "law of order" in realizing God consciousness. That law states that Cosmic consciousness must be in place before Christ consciousness. The traditional method is to attain levels of Christ consciousness in the 5D, and work through them for a period of time, which can consume many lifetimes for the Soul. For most this is an impossible task. Eventually 5D Christ consciousness is transcended in favor of Cosmic consciousness. This allows the re-emergence of Christ consciousness through the 7D, which is the first level of God consciousness.

---

[1] Hidden or behind the scenes.

[2] General rather than specific.

The question then becomes, how do we get through the 5D without getting trapped inside those levels of Christ consciousness? One answer is to transcend the 5D through the accumulation of balanced pairs of chakras. This raises additional questions of where to start and which centers balance each other[3].

In Time Traveler methodology, there are two necessary operations that need to be observed, they are:

1. The necessity of starting at the very center of our being, and;

2. The necessity of activating paired polar opposite chakras in a certain definite order.

The reason we need to activate paired chakras is that each pair of polarized chakras neutralize one another, resulting in an accumulation of chakras resulting in the expansion of the indwelling self[4]. In other words, by using this method, we can effectively move completely through the fifth dimension by *expansion* of the indwelling self to exceed in size the physical body and exit the 5D into the 6D without having to experiencing 5D Christ consciousness while at the same time accumulating it as part of the 6D structure[5]. This is the result of neutralizing the effects of the 5D through observing the paradoxes of balanced chakras.

We start at the Heart center because it is the vibrational middle of the color spectrum (green). It is then a simple matter of moving one level at a time away from the center (both up and down the color scale), which results in matching the polar opposites. For example:

1. The Throat chakra (blue) and Upper Solar Plexus chakra (dark yellow or pink).

2. The Mouth (indigo) and Lower Solar Plexus chakras (bright yellow).

3. The Third Eye (purple) and Splenic (orange) chakras.

---

[3] A reminder, we are avoiding the flywheel effect by using counterbalancing expansion techniques rather than traditional linear methods.

[4] The indwelling self is usually about the size of a ping-pong ball in most people.

[5] Remember that the 6D is comprised of 6 separate dimensions. Once they are blended, they become the 6D.

4. The Crown (violet) and Pubic (dark red) chakras, and finally we pair

5. The Top of the Head (ultra violet) and Coccyx (infrared) chakras.

Obviously this could not work with the old seven chakra system now in vogue.

Meditation

1. We start by first warming up the Heart Center, as described in earlier meditations.

2. Next, we extend our meditation by falling or relaxing back one level (floating up or inward) to include the Throat Center while, at the same time, moving outward in effort (pushing outward or down) to include the Upper Solar Plexus, as described in the last Chapter. This dual motion of *inward* (relaxation or opposite of trying) and *outward* is something that needs to be mastered for the 5D meds to be of any significance. Although it might appear a bit daunting at first, with practice it becomes quite natural and easy.

3. Next, we stimulate the Mouth Center by toning the note of MI. As we sound the note Mi (ME) feel the resonate vibration reflect into the Upper and Lower Solar Plexus. This is a natural result and should produce anything from good feelings to bliss in the solar plexus region. This is also good for calming anger.

You can experiment with toning if you care to. DO vibrates the Heart Center. Descending scale, DO, TI, LA, where TI vibrates the Upper Solar Plexus and can be used in conjunction with that meditation, for calming anxiety and fear.

Once you feel that the fifth dimensional Heart Center is open from the Mouth to the Lower Solar Plexus, visualize it as a powerful and bright shining and radiant white light that others can sense. Feel its radiance and increasing warmth easily melt your problems and illness away. Feel and see its healing effects upon you and all of those around you.

As an aside, below are the tones of the musical scale and their corresponding centers. You can actually feel these individual centers vibrate as you tone.

Ascending Scale

(6) LA—Top of the Head
(5) SO—Crown
(4) FA—Third Eye
(3) MI—Mouth
(2) RE—Throat
(1) DO—Heart

Descending Scale

(1) DO—Heart
(2) TI—Upper Solar Plexus
(3) LA—Lower Solar Plexus
(4) SO—Splenic
(5) FA—Pubic
(6) MI—Coccyx

This concludes this Chapter. In the next Chapter we will examine in detail the techniques and results of opening up the The Third Eye and the Splenic Centers.

CHAPTER 27

FIFTH DIMENSIONAL MEDITATION: EXERCISE FIVE

The centers we will open in this Chapter are the *Between the Eyes Center*, also called the *Third Eye*[1], and the *Splenic Center*[2]. The color of the Between the Eyes Center is purple. It is the center of will-power and concentration. People who use this center are noted for their tenacity and focus.

The color of the Splenic Center is orange. It is the center that produces our physical life force. It has been mistakenly called the Sexual Center because of spontaneous orgasms experienced by women when it is opened by practitioners after a long period of being closed. This center is responsible for physical vitality and when shut down, forces the individual to substitute sexual energy in its place. This in turn causes marital problems such as "Business man's impotency" and hyper activity in women. The vital orange energy gives a person a zest for life and a desire to actively participate. The problems that occur when this center is not balanced by its counterpart[3] are manic in nature. By this I mean a person will exhibit various levels of having to constantly do something. When left unchecked, it can result in nervous disorders, such as ADD and manic behavior.

Orange energy, when used by a balanced person, provides a nice endless energy that is almost invisible. In other words, it is not hard on the nervous system, while being wonderfully effective. Many women purposely shut this center down in the work place for reasons of professionalism. This forms a sort of sexual chastity belt which consequently adversely affects the sex life of a large number of women.

The counterpart to the orange center is the purple center at the Third Eye. The overuse of purple energy can give rise to anything from extreme seriousness and intensity to mood swings and melancholia.

In this meditation, we will learn to properly combine these two

---

[1] Located between the two eyes.

[2] Called this because of its supposed association with the spleen. It is located between the Lower Solar Plexus and the Pubic Center.

[3] The Third Eye.

centers to form an ideal combination.

Meditation (Review)

1. We start by first warming up the Heart Center as described in earlier meditations.

2. Next, we extend our meditation by expanding to include the Throat and the Upper Solar Plexus, as described in Chapter 25.

3. Next, we stimulate the Mouth Center by toning the note of MI. As we sound the note Mi (ME), feel the resonate vibration in the Lower Solar Plexus. This is a natural result and should produce anything from good feelings to bliss in the Lower Solar Plexus.

4. Next feel that the fifth dimensional Heart Center is open from the Mouth to the Lower Solar Plexus. Visualize it as a powerful and bright shining and radiant white light with a slight golden tint.

Additional Meditation Technique

Next, tap the spot between your eyes to wake it up. Do this with your eyes closed. Visualize a point of white light directly in front of you. When you have done this, gently massage the orange center until you feel both centers blend into and extend the Heart Center from the Third Eye to just above the Pubic Center.

The results of this meditation are very subtle and increase over time. It will safely give you access to focus and tenacity while also infusing you with boundless but easy energy. You will gradually feel an intensification of bliss and love.

The more you do the meditations, the more dramatic will be the results. This soon becomes very noticeable in the residual effects as you move through your daily routine. It will take the form of intensified interaction with others, and noticeably increased energy. Some people might experience excess energy and possibly some problems sleeping in the beginning, but this will normalize in a week or two.

This concludes this Chapter. In the next Chapter we will examine in detail the techniques and results of opening up the Crown and Pelvic centers.

CHAPTER 28

FIFTH DIMENSIONAL MEDITATION: EXERCISE SIX

In this Chapter we will examine a technique for achieving the addition of pairing the *Crown* and *Pubic* centers to our growing list.

We are rapidly approaching the end of the *Fifth Dimensional Meditations*. In order to progress beyond these into the next level, we need to master the meditations as presented. There comes a time for us when we must decide whether we are serious about what we are attempting to do here. If we are not serious in our intent, then there will be a tendency not to take the meditations seriously as well. You can tell if this is happening to you if you find even the most frivolous demands of the 3D world more important than making time for the meditations.

I mention this because it is a subtle form of drawing you back into the karma of the third dimension and back to sleep. If you really want to awaken and break out of the hard 3D egg shell in which you are imprisoned, then you must fight for it with all of your strength to crack that shell and emerge into the universal light. A lackadaisical effort will yield a lackadaisical result. Remember that if this was an easy task, we would all have done it by now.

The Crown chakra is known as the thousand-petaled lotus. It encircles the head like a band crossing the forehead area. Access to this center opens tremendous levels of clairvoyant knowledge, power and abilities, not the least which is the transmutation of sexual energy into a creative force.

The sexual chakra or Pubic center is renowned for its potential problems, if left to its own devices. These two centers, when merged and brought to full capacity, have produced many dark wizards of old (and new). When merged with all of the other centers, they become a power structure for transmuting sexual energy into the spiritual gold of the true healer.

Meditation (Review)

1. We start by first warming up the Heart Center, as described in earlier meditations.

2. Next, we extend our meditation by expanding to include the Throat and the Upper Solar Plexus, as described in Chapter 25.

3. Next, we stimulate the Mouth Center by toning the note of MI. As we sound the note Mi (ME) feel the resonate vibration in the Lower Solar Plexus. This is a natural result and should produce anything from good feelings to bliss in the Lower Solar Plexus.

4. Nex,t feel that the fifth dimensional Heart Center is open from the Mouth to the Lower Solar Plexus. Visualize it as a powerful and bright shining and radiant white light with a slight golden tint.

5. Next, tap the spot between your eyes to wake it up. Do this with your eyes closed. Visualize a point of white light directly in front of you. When you have done this, gently massage the orange center[1] until you feel both centers blend into and extend the Heart Center from the Third Eye to just above the Pubic Center.

Additional Meditation Technique

Next, with eyes closed, place both palms of your hands on the sides of your head just above the temples. Feel and see the energy from your hands stimulate this center. After a moment, slowly move your hands away from your head to a distance of between 6 to 12 inches depending on what feel best for you. As you move your hands slowly away from your head, feel and see the energy within the Crown Center begin to glow and vibrate. Feel the power hidden there begin to come awake.

Once you have done this to the best of your ability, feel the counterbalancing force of the Sexual Center begin to vibrate. Rather than feeling sexual, it should blend in with the other centers in the form of radiant power and good feelings. If you are not feeling anything,

---

[1] Located in the front of the body, between the Lower Solar Plexus and the Pubic Center.

make sure that you are spending enough time opening each center and especially that your Heart Center is as warm as you can make it[2].

This concludes this Chapter. In the next Chapter, we will examine in detail the techniques and results of opening up the Top of the Head Center and Anal Center.

---

[2] A circular or light scratching motion at the small indentation at the center of your chest will help warm this chakra up.

CHAPTER 29

FIFTH DIMENSIONAL MEDITATION:
EXERCISE SEVEN

This is the last in the series of *Fifth Dimensional Meditations*. The Chapter after this one will take us into the pure Sixth Dimension.

Review

I feel that another review is in order to make sure we are ready for these last few steps in this section. We are multidimensional beings in the transitional phase. This means we are not yet what we will be. We have been experiencing a level of reality that is far less than we are capable of experiencing. There is nothing wrong with this level. It is very much like a play pen or safe area for children. Children are not yet what they will be. They experience a level of reality that is far less demanding than that which they will experience in adulthood. We put them in play pens for their own safety. However, there comes a time when the child outgrows the play pen and is ready for greater levels of experience and responsibility.

The difference between the reality we consider as "normal" and a multidimensional reality is encapsulated as follows:

1. In a normal reality, we experience time as *forward* motion in the form of instantaneous time slices. We are usually denied access to previous or future existence.

2. In multidimensional reality, we experience time as a universal *now* where everything that ever happened or ever will happen is happening all at once[1].

In our normal 3D existence we experience life in a segmented fashion, like individual frames on a roll of film. When we die, we experience our 11 bodies one after the other as it each lives out its life and dies. We ascend in ever higher octaves of vibration until we finally shed the

---

[1] This is not confusing to us in a multidimensional reality because these myriad separate events are homogenized in a very wonderful way that promotes a perfection of being.

highest vibrational body, only to find ourselves back in physical reality as a new born baby, bereft of our previous memory.

In multidimensional reality, we understand that all experience—including birth and death—goes on un-noticed within and beneath the surface of the unified self, very much like the renewing cell structure in our physical bodies goes on un-noticed by us. We are, at the aggregate Soul level, literally a composite of eons of 3D lifetimes. Each lifetime is a miniature experience, necessary as a tiny part of multidimensional reality. We can think of each lifetime as a piece of a large puzzle. Each piece is relatively insignificant as compared to the completed puzzle, but very noticeable and conspicuous if missing.

We are structured in such a marvelous way that out of virtually unlimited possibility, we experience only exactly what we are ready for. Our belief structures dictate precisely what our realities will be at any given moment.

Wherever we find ourselves in the unbounded possibilities of creation, we have at our command equal access to multidimensional existence. It is always right there ready for discovery. The steps necessary to achieve it are exactly the same for everyone. It is my hope that by outlining and practicing these steps we may clarify a viable and easily accessible path to multidimensional freedom, which others may follow if they choose to pursue it.

Meditation (Review)

1. We start by first warming up the Heart Center, as described in earlier meditations.

2. Next, we extend our meditation by expanding to include the Throat and the Upper Solar Plexus, as described in Chapter 25.

3. Next, we stimulate the Mouth Center by toning the note of MI. As we sound the note Mi (ME) feel the resonate vibration in the Lower Solar Plexus. This is a natural result and should produce anything from good feelings to bliss in the Lower Solar Plexus.

4. Next feel the Heart Center opening from the Mouth to the Lower Solar Plexus. Visualize it as a powerful and bright shining and radiant white light with a slight golden tint.

5. Next, tap the spot between your eyes to wake it up. Do this with your eyes closed. Visualize a point of white light directly in front

of you. When you have done this, gently massage the orange center[2] until you feel both centers blend into and extend the Heart center from the Third Eye to just above the Pubic center.

6. Next, with eyes closed, place both palms of your hands on the sides of your head just above the temples. Feel and see the energy from your hands stimulate this center. After a moment, slowly move your hands away from your head to a distance of between 6 to 12 inches depending on what feel best for you. As you move your hands slowly away from your head, feel and see the energy within the crown center begin to glow and vibrate. Feel the power hidden there begin to come awake.

Once you have done this to the best of your ability, feel the counterbalancing force of the sexual center begin to vibrate. Rather than feeling sexual, it should blend in with the other centers in the form of radiant power and good feelings. If you are not feeling anything, make sure that you are spending enough time opening each center.

Additional Meditation Technique

Find a spot at the very top and center of your head. By massaging this spot you will activate this center. This is the *Prudent Body* responsible for controlling the energy flow through all 11 bodies. The Prudent Body, if malfunctioning, can produce inordinate fear and mental disorders such as paranoia. It also, in conjunction with the Upper Solar Plexus, can set off anxiety attacks and bouts of acid reflux.

This body, when working properly with the other 10[3], is counterbalanced by the physical body whose center is called the *Coccyx* or *Anal* center, located as where the name might indicate.

The physical body by itself is bereft of even a personality. Without the benefit of the higher bodies, the physical body is concerned only with bodily functions. You probably know people who are overly preoccupied with their physical bodies. They usually have nick names like "Meat" and "Vanity".

---

[2] Located in the front of the body between the Lower Solar Plexus and the Pubic Center.

[3] The reason we each have only 11 chakras instead of 12 is that the Sexual Center comprises two separate centers. Red-Aries for a man and Burgundy-Virgo for a woman.

We have seen each pair of polarized bodies as we have progressed through the meditation, but this polarity of the Prudent and Physical bodies is particularly unique in that both bodies interface with the *void*. The physical body interfaces with the *outside* 3D world. It is a physical boundary that keeps you from spilling out into space. The prudent body also interfaces with space, but it is with *inside* space that is found to reside inside of your 11 bodies as "inner space", a place separate from, but occupying the same space as physical form. In other words, it is a place in the same space as you occupy now, but as space where you do not (cannot) exist. When we observe the three dimensions of outer space plus the three dimensions of inner space, we have the Sixth Dimension, which we will examine in detail in the next Chapter.

As was mentioned before, by massaging the Top of the Head Center, it can be activated. There is a high pitched whistle associated with this center. You may or may not "hear" this whistle. You may also feel a localized pressure or energy at the spot at the top of your head.

Once you feel that you have sufficiently stimulated this center, become aware of the Anal center. This will sensitize your physical body. The net result we are looking for is to expand the heart center to completely engulf the 11 bodies, extending from the most inner and highest vibrational to the most outer and lowest vibrational body.

This is the completed Fifth dimension. Please do not look for anything spectacular to happen at this point. You may or may not feel any different. This doesn't matter. There is nothing we want to use here at this time. The Fifth dimension is the heart of the physical structure and is meant to be transcended in tact.

We have not reached the point of "no return" yet, and even at this greatly expanded state there is a danger of falling back in the form of the "Savior Complex". In fact this is the most dangerous point in this regard. Remember that the Fifth Dimensional Meditation is designed to access fifth dimensional Christ consciousness without being trapped within it. The result is truly the difference between the covered wagon and the jet plane. The importance of putting off Christ consciousness until at least the Seventh dimension is fundamental to Time Traveler principles.

This concludes this Chapter. In the next Chapter we will step out into the pure Sixth Dimension.

Chapter 30

Sixth Dimensional Meditation:
Exercise One

In this Chapter we are about to leave the Fifth dimension altogether. In order to do this we must be willing to leave behind much of what we consider as being human. This step will separate the ones of you who are ready to go on and those who need more life times to complete your karmic debts.

We have experienced the Fifth dimension as a viewpoint that expands both internally and externally in balanced vibrational polar opposites. Before we started the 5D series of meditations, we experienced our bodies as a golf ball sized center of energy. This limited our experience to a single center at a time.

At the conclusion of these meditations we have expanded to encompass the entire body. The composite Fifth dimension exists in time and space as our Heart Center. It is not meant to be lived in as such. We are only half way in our journey. We need to proceed on into the blackness of the Sixth Dimensional void, for out of the blackness comes the light.

Meditation

We can access the 6D by performing the *Fifth Dimensional Meditations* described in the previous Chapters. In the last Chapter we reached a place where we were expanded from the Top of the Head Center—which resonates with the inner most and highest vibratory body—to the Anal Center—which resonates with the outer most and lowest vibratory body.

Once you have reached this expanded state, the next step is to move inward into the space within your being while moving out into the physical space around you. It means completely letting go of your physical form internally while at the same time expanding out beyond your physical body. This allows you to experience existence from outside of your form.

As you expand beyond the confines of your composite 5D body, you realize that you are looking at yourself from the outside. However, this outside also includes the extreme inside where form no longer can exist. In other words, you realize that there is a void in the very space you occupy.

There are three dimensions of outside space and three dimensions of inside space existing as polar opposites. Suspended in-between this composite space is what you call your physical form. As you look at it you see it has changed and is no longer the Fifth dimension, but has metamorphosed into the Seventh dimension. It was the 5D as long as we were expanding within it. This is the nature of the 5D viewpoint.

The 6D is the 5D with one more dimension added to it. Its nature and view point is from the composite outside. As we begin to interact with the former 5D, we realize that we cannot re-enter the form, but must operate it from the 6D. This gives us a permanent buffer that will keep us from falling back into the 5D. In other words, by controlling the 5D from the 6D, the 5D becomes an additional dimension or the Seventh dimension. This is your *Stellar Body*, the physical vehicle for your soon to arrive *Future Self*.

Seventh Dimensional Expectations

The first thing we notice about the 7D is that it comes from within the center of our being. It is a brilliant white that is expanding or shining out through us into the void. It has a crisp and clean crystalline feeling and appearance and is the source of consummate bliss. There is a fine line that must be observed between being drawn into the bliss only to wind up back in the 5D and maintaining the uncaringness (another kind of bliss) of the 6D while learning how to operate in this fashion. The change is subtle and natural. As the bliss increases day by day, we will need to put it in motion out to others in the form of love. This is the golden Eight dimension.

This concludes this Chapter. In the next Chapter we will delve more deeply into the interaction between the Sixth and Seventh dimensions.

CHAPTER 31

SIXTH DIMENSIONAL MEDITATION: REVIEW

Here in the 6D we have reached a natural barrier to our progress. In order to proceed on into the Seventh dimension we need to be done with the 5D and all of its individual component parts. We are learning on a three level tier, i.e. knowing, being, and doing.

The *knowing* part is the information your Soul has accumulated through countless life times of hard work, and augmented by the Chapters to help bring the essential points to your present physical mind in this time period. The *doing* part is your taking action to make change an active part of your daily life. The *being* part are the rewards you reap for all of your long labors as you forever become more wonderful and beautiful and powerful.

From a larger perspective, we are following the path laid down by the original creative consciousness[1] as it made its way from the primordial cradle to where you stand now and beyond. There was a time that consciousness transcended time and space and realized that there was only one consciousness manifesting in all of time and space through all created form. It realized that all experience belonged to it. That it was the creator and the created. There came a blinding flash of realization that united all consciousness and form wherever it may reside in existence. No matter how removed or corrupted the form and entrapped consciousness had become, it was found and guided into perfection. No one is lost and this most certainly includes *you.*

The most important element in all of this to that founding consciousness was the quality of *free will.* Consciousness realized that it was duplicating itself through an infinite variety of individualized experience, and in order for it to manifest in its special uniqueness, it had to be free to choose the time and place it would eventually be set free to merge with the perfected collective.

This time and place would naturally occur when the individual consciousness was willing to transcend its physical form in perfect faith and trust that there was a higher power leading and guiding it

---

[1] I choose to call it my *Time Traveling Oversoul.*

through each life time and each experience until it stood at the brink, face to face with the void, willing to fall like a child into the loving arms of a parent, knowing that very close, just beyond the void, was the face of God, and that somehow it was *you*.

We are about to usher in "Heaven on Earth". It will happen just as fast as you can stand it. Or just as slowly as you want it to be. It doesn't have to happen in this lifetime or in a thousand lifetimes if you don't want it to.

Almost all of the work we are doing is a letting go of preconceived ideas of who we are. If you are too afraid to let go, then perhaps it will not happen in this lifetime for you. You will not know if others have re-entered the Garden of Eden or not because your perception will not allow you to be where they are. If you choose to continue to live in illusion then illusion will be your reality. The universe creates your illusions to form fit your consciousness. Your life and everything in it is exactly what you have created according to your belief system and the quality of being you choose to manifest. Illusion is absolute. Anything you choose to believe to preserve your illusionary world will spring forth as unwavering proof that you are right. Such is the absoluteness of illusion.

Remember that nothing is impossible. If you allow miracles into your world, then miracles will happen.

CHAPTER 32

SIXTH DIMENSIONAL MEDITATION: EXERCISE TWO

Part of the Sixth to Seventh dimensional transitional work we must do is to balance the future/past into a unified *Now*. Many people spend a terrific amount of time either in the future or the past. In conversation they will tell you about their day or their week or how it was in 1942. Other times people will give elaborate and detailed plans about how they are going to look or be or have in the future. Very few people are right here in the now with you.

You might be aware of your own tendency to drift into the past or future. There is nothing wrong with this because we need to learn from the past and plan in the future. However, because of our desire to progress beyond "normal" 3D existence, it has become necessary for us to learn to function from the Six dimensional "Now".

The 6D *Now* transcends time and yet allows us access to the future and the past at the same time as a *universal Now*. This is part of the awakening process. Our goal is to travel from all time to the present. This is why it is called *time travel*.

To accomplish living in the *Now* takes a good deal of effort and practice. You cannot access the enlightenment and bliss of the seventh dimension (and beyond) unless you have mastered how to be in the *Now*.

Those of you who are already making efforts to stay in the *Now* are most likely aware of the deadening effect people who are not in the "now" have upon you. This can be avoided by using the detachment of the 6D. In other words, instead of allowing a person who is chronically in the past/future to pull down on your consciousness like an anchor, there is a technique you can use. When confronted by a 3D future/past person, let them wander in time, but don't allow yourself to wander with them. In other words, observe what they are doing as a study of what not to do. Stay in present time at all costs. This will allow you to see where people are in time. I think it may amaze you.

Meditation

Start by doing a complete 5D meditation. If you have been practicing, you should be getting good at this by now. Once all of your centers are vibrating, begin the 6D meditation by transcending the 5D and accessing the 6D void.

Once you feel a sufficient detachment from your 5D form, center your consciousness in the *Now*. Float in present time. Detach from the chatter of your mind. Detach from the urgency of your emotions. Focus upon objects in your environment. Listen to yourself breath. Look at your hands. Avoid thinking or making judgments. Go outside and look at a tree or a plant, avoid thinking what kind of tree or plant it is. See it as unique and as a living thing that is here in the *Now* with you. If you have an animal look at it, not as a cat or a dog or as Fluffy or Duke, but as a living thing that is here in the *Now* with you.

Be aware that you are alive and aware. If you encounter another person, see them as a living being that is here in the *Now* with you. They may ask you what is wrong? Smile and stay in the meditation. Do this meditation only for a few minutes to start with, but do it at least once a day. Then gradually increase the amount of time.

CHAPTER 33

SIXTH DIMENSIONAL MEDITATION: DISCUSSION

The Sixth dimension has several levels to work through, just as we have seen in previous dimensions. The 6D and 7D have long been sought after in the Eastern metaphysical disciplines. These are known as the Buddhic and Nirvanic planes respectively. Many advanced Yoga techniques are devoted to attaining these goals, and the reasons and techniques were wonderfully covered by Patanjali in the Yoga Sutras. However, the problem with these techniques is they are very time-consuming and difficult. They were not designed for the modern Western mind. We like fast and easy. We also like *safe*.

That we need to take the trip is not in question, but why take a covered wagon when we can take a jet? Almost all of the work that is to be done by us in achieving the 6th and 7th dimensions entail letting go of attachments and misconceptions on other dimensions, while at the same time maintaining the foundations of those dimensions. It is important to remember that we need to transcend each dimension while at the same time retaining it. This is the formula for the successful accumulation of each dimension rather than simply transcending them through detachment in stair step fashion.

In order to obtain the serenity of the 6D, we must change or eliminate some of the preconceived ideas found in the 5D. In addition to this, we must thoroughly let go of the emotional attachments found in the 4D, and last but certainly not least, we must modify the 3D habit of having to *do* something every minute.

If we look closely, perhaps we can find a common denominator which underlies the reasons why we are saddled with these impediments to begin with. Finding such a common denominator might easily compress our chore of attaining the 6D into fast and easy (and safe). That common denominator, as you might have guessed, is *fear*[1].

Most of us are afraid of something, and some of us are afraid of everything. We have good reason to be afraid for we live in a very

---

[1] For those of you who thought boredom was the common denominator, boredom is usually just the result of being afraid to try something new.

scary time and place. Our mind may tell us that we are not afraid, or our pride might not allow us to believe we are afraid, but down deep we *all* fear something. Our biggest fear is usually the fear of the unknown. If we encounter something that is unknown, our imaginations can run rampant, often producing unreasonable fear. We are walking down a dark street and we hear an unfamiliar noise, we will most likely become fearful.

How can we overcome this fear of the unknown? One obvious way is by simply making it known. Afraid of the dark? Turn on the light and usually the fear goes away. A strange noise on a dark street? We see a dog rummaging in a trash can. No more fear. Likewise, by examining the 6D void and becoming familiar with it, hopefully most of our fear of it will gradually be eliminated.

We have reached a point in our studies where, afraid or not, we must venture into the void. This is very scary for most of us. It fills us with dread, but in order to proceed, we have to master it. Some of us might get the same feeling as if someone has asked us to jump off of a tall building. No manner of reassurance is going to temp you. Even if the person asking you to jump has jumped off of the building many times with impunity or if thousands of people have jumped right before your eyes and landed safely, you are still going to have some questions. What if it works for them but not for me? What if this is just an illusion or a delusion? What if...what if...what if...

To continue with the tall building analogy, what if it was explained to you that these people had bungy cords or parachutes? This would put jumping into a different light altogether. You still might not be tempted to jump, but at least you would begin to understand that it is possible to jump and not get hurt.

The next level of removing fear might be to convince you that out of thousands and thousands of people who have jumped, there was not one single person hurt. You still might not jump until you found out that jumping was the only way down, and that the building was on fire. Some of us would still not jump, but we might be seriously considering it at this point.

What we are attempting to accomplish is not nearly as dangerous as jumping from a tall building. In fact it is not dangerous at all. There are built in safety factors that prevent us from moving too fast just as a baby is safe in its playpen, we are exploring the unlimited side of our nature *when we are ready*. If we are not ready, then we find that we *cannot do it.* It is really very simple. Those of us who are ready are gathering together to help each other through our mutual fears so we may enjoy our birthright. Our Souls have worked non stop through endless lifetimes to reach this point. Our desire and excitement is far greater than our fear because we have already worked through most of our fear.

What we are doing is much more than mere intellectual speculation or theory. Those of you who are excited and motivated to a point of impatience know what I am talking about. Those of you who are too afraid to take a chance or too lazy to make an effort probably do not belong here. This is a class for spiritual adults who are making final preparations to shed the cocoon and emerge as magnificent God like creatures so different from what and where they were as to be practically unrecognizable.

There are those of you who do not know why you are here. You are afraid but you are attracted like the proverbial "moth to the flame". It is you to whom most of the work here is directed, for I understand your predicament. We are motivated from within our very souls. We have no choice but to proceed regardless of how scary or impossible it may seem. We might be hesitant and clumsy in our first attempts much like we were when we were babies and first tried to walk, but walk we must because it is our *destiny*.

In order for us to begin to live we must first be willing to let go of the fear of dying.

CHAPTER 34

THE SIXTH DIMENSION
(CONT.)

The Sixth Dimension is the great leveler. It is the place where you must stand naked before universal consciousness. You are not able to take anything with you except your faith. It is the stem of the hour glass between the past and the future. It is here that not only do you come face to face with the void, but that you also become it.

The 6D void can be a place of great joy and adventure, unlike the 1D void, which is a place of nothingness and—for a human being—a place of utter dread. We come into the 6D still full of self-centeredness and fear. Self-centeredness must gradually be replaced with a willingness to share our growing consciousness with other beings through wisdom and balance and unconditional love. A natural balance of give and take. Sharing and yet maintaining autonomy.

We must be willing to replace fear with an unmitigated and consummate faith in a Higher Power. This faith in a Higher Power must never waiver, for in order to let go on such a monumental scale, faith is all that you can take with you. "I pray only for knowledge of God's will for me and the power to carry that out".

For some of you the awakening will be instantaneous. For others it will be a slow and gradual happening. It may not all happen for you in this lifetime. This is perfectly all right. Each lifetime has led your Soul closer to Its goals. This lifetime has put you on the brink.

Be kind to yourself. You cannot make a flower grow faster or become more beautiful by beating it. Have fun as you grow so that we may have fun and grow *together*.

This concludes the section on the Sixth Dimension. In the next Chapter we will examine the 7th dimension and some of the traps found there.

CHAPTER 35

SEVENTH DIMENSIONAL TRAPS

In the Chapters prior to this one, we have been working from viewpoints involving the *old* self working to allow the new self to manifest. From this Chapter on, we will be working as the *new* self, resolving the karmic problems found in this incarnation and in this time period, in order to facilitate our further involvement.

Accepting responsibility as a Seventh Dimensional Being is very great and yet very simple. At this point in our sojourn, we are still neither the old or the new. We are still at the null point between two worlds. However, we are shifting the idea of who we are from someone who is trapped inside of time wanting to be free, to someone who is already free and wishes to manifest here from outside of time.

We bring with us tremendous knowledge and power, but it will take time and patience for us to fully realize this. We need to understand that we are now much more responsible for our thoughts and actions than ever before, existing in a kind of "instant karma" where everything you do and think manifests very quickly. This is particularly noticeable if your actions are negative.

In the 7D, illusion still persists. There will be a tendency to think you have transcended illusion, but this is a mistake. Although we have entered the Nirvanic realms—thought by many as the ultimate goal—it is only just past the half way point for us and we must use caution to be able to get through this part. There are several traps that can impede your progress which need to be explained.

Traps

There are two major traps to be aware of are:

1. Slipping back into the Fifth dimension while thinking you are progressing in the Seventh dimension.

2. Slipping into the Second dimension (white light) in a schizoid break from reality.

The first trap, slipping back into the Fifth dimension, is something that needs to be monitored constantly in the beginning. The reason for this phenomenon is the inadvertent letting go of the 6D. Remember that these dimensions—or view points—are brought together by a process of accumulation. This means we must maintain all of the component parts. To do otherwise is to degenerate into lesser positions in consciousness.

In the *Six Dimensional Meditations*, we learned that we were forming a "time portal" from which we could await the arrival of our Oversoul in order to form the 7D merger. The 6D provides a certain aloofness that prevents us from shifting our center back into the past incarnations ego, and this aloofness or "serenity" must be maintained from now on.

The accumulation of an additional dimension, or view point, to realize that the 7D depends upon the maintenance of those previously accrued six component dimensions. In other words, especially with the advent of the 7D, it is necessary to maintain a state of not caring about it. This dichotomy is a trade mark of God consciousness.

The 7D carries with it emotional capabilities and experience far beyond anything we have ever felt. To care or desire simply prevents the 7D from happening at all or at the very least degrades our experience into something far less than 7D. Our ability to not care and to let go dictates how fast we will be able to begin to experience the 7D.

Your goal of preserving the past incarnation's ego and working through it with its full knowledge and cooperation is at hand with the advent of the 7D. In order to do this without falling back into the past is a balancing trick that must be mastered, not an easy task in this lead weighted reality where everyone and everything seems to exist for the sole purpose of putting you back to sleep. You can attempt to stay awake and aware that the possibility exists for you to degenerate. If you can work with others who are also "waking up", then you can remind each other to stay 6D.

The second trap, slipping into the white light state of the Primordial Second dimension, which we will designate as the "2D"[1], although it is the ultimate goal for many, produces a separation in consciousness that, although temporary, may be difficult to reverse in this lifetime, given the fact that it appears as though something exceedingly great and wonderful has happened. This is the result of a letting go of the component dimensions comprising the 6D rather than maintaining

---

[1] Not to be confused with the 2D, which interfaces with the personality housed in the Sexual body.

their accumulation.

The realization of white light for us is the accumulation of seven separate dimensions brought into one. Although the Seventh dimension and the Primordial Second dimension are very similar in the respect that they both produce a white light state in the consciousness of the seeker, the similarity stops there. The 2D is nothing but white light without any divisions or shades of difference. Many call this God or Heaven. Returning to the 2D is, in fact, the ultimate returning to the womb, back to the beginning before creation. This may sound like what you have always been seeking, but it seems—at least to me—to be a complete reversal of the "Universal intent" of manifestation.

What precautions can be taken to prevent this, and how will we know if it has occurred? In the nature of precautions, paramount is the avoidance of desiring the 7D. We learned in the 6D that cessation of desire while working in the world as though we cared intently, was necessary to maintain 6D serenity.

Wanting to experience the "white light" state can set in motion a 2D white light state. This is the state most if not all mystics experience when so intently and systematically seeking the higher levels of Nirvana. The solution is to routinely maintain 6D patience concerning the 7D. Giving up to your Oversoul means exactly that. It is up to your Oversoul when and if you will experience the 7D and whether it will even happen in this lifetime or not.

Desire is a creative tool to be later used by your future self for creative purposes. As a final word, you technically already possess the 7D. All you need to do is a sufficient letting go for a sufficient amount of time to realize it. To desire something you already possess invariably has the result of denying it.

Do not expect too much of yourself now. It is common—at least in my experience—at this point to alternate back and forth between the component dimensions of the 7D. Simply be aware of it when you do. By not being overly concerned, this normal but often disconcerting oscillation will eventually subside. Set aside a little time each day to do the meditation techniques. This will help you stay awake. Remember that you are no longer in control. All that will happen, will happen in God's time. We can only be a ready and willing participant.

CHAPTER 36

SEVENTH DIMENSIONAL MEDITATIONS

The Seventh dimension, as previously stated, is the first plateau of God consciousness for us. The 7D gives you access to the first of three God-like qualities. The first is being-ness in the form of bliss and enlightenment. The second quality, found in the Eight dimension, is universal love and knowing-ness. The third quality, doing-ness, is wisdom and power, not found until the Ninth dimension and is not fully mastered until the Tenth.

As amazingly wonderful as these dimensions are as they each are added unto you, you are still *alone* in your universe and subject to delusions in the form of divine paranoia. It is important to remember that whether it looks like it or not, we are all equal. *Everyone* is your peer outside of time as you are currently experiencing it. Even the seemingly most unlikely person is your equal. This is not simply a nice sentiment, it is a prime rule that must be understood and practiced. Without this kind of balance in your universe, you will have little chance of maintaining your new found level of experience.

We are still subject to the laws of illusion and must make every effort to blend in and act to the outside world as though we were exactly the same as we were before we started the 7D merger. This is very important and tricky. It will not only keep you out of the funny farm, it will also bring much less resistance to you in the form of a kind of instant karma from spouses, friends and loved ones. We are in a time period that is still—by Time Traveler standards—in the middle of the "Dark Ages". Fraught with witch hunts and superstition, anything people do not understand is labeled as Satanic or Cultist. The less that is said about what is happening to you, the better.

What will shine through is a new glow that people will comment on. Yourself from the future is here with you now. What you are experiencing, it is experiencing. What concerns it at this time is how to turn the light switch on without blinding everyone. Remember that enlightenment is a team effort. What effects one effects all. The difficulty with approaching this physical dimension is if the approach is too fast or sudden, it makes a negative result.

There is a critical point (where you should be right now if you have been diligent in practicing these techniques) where your consciousness literally begins to turn inside out and radiate white light out into the 3D. With it comes a powerful surge of emotional energy. For some, there may be a sudden rush of wonderful feelings, while for others there will be a gradual increase of light and good feelings coming from within the center of their being. The problem is if you are not properly prepared for it, you may scare the hell out of everyone around you. Yourself from the future has not gone to this much trouble to merge with you, only to have you become too unstable to manage it.

The challenge here is, no matter how wonderful you may feel, try to act normally. See if you can experience all that is happening to you without talking about it to anyone. Like the controlled chain reaction in a nuclear power plant, you must learn how to control it or it will quickly overwhelm you.

By sitting on it you act as a damper that will make it work for you. It is only natural to want to share your new found feelings with those around you. This is love…but do it quietly. If you suddenly start blessing everyone and hollering "Ureka. I have found it.", obviously this could cause more problems than you might care to have.

"Yourself" from the future has certain valid concerns about manifesting here through you and thus into the lower six dimensions. After all, acknowledging these concerns and displaying trust, openness and willingness is really all that can be expected of you…and that you might welcome it with all of your heart.

CHAPTER 37

SEVENTH DIMENSIONAL MEDITATIONS

As you make the transition to the first levels of the Seventh dimension, your understanding of yourself and the universe will begin to flower. The fearful and cloistered self-centered closed-mindedness of the old self will begin to fade away. We are graduating from the sub-atomic to the atomic. From earth-centered consciousness to solar-centered consciousness. From random and remote pieces and time slices of ourselves to a unified self in time and space, confident of its place in the universe.

In the beginning it may seem that there is little or no difference in your consciousness, but it is like a tiny crack in a giant dam. At first, only a few drops of water appear and then a little more, until a noticeable stream develops. Eventually and inevitably, a great torrent pushes its way through the opening with a thunderous roar.

In the beginning, out of fearful preservation we may try to stop the flow of consciousness, but it is not ours to stop. This would be akin to the caterpillar trying to stop its metamorphoses to a butterfly. We are metamorphic beings. This means that we change from one state of being to another. It is simply part of our nature. We can put off this change by recycling back through time until we are ready to proceed, but once we pass the point of no return we are committed to go on the next stage. If you feel you are ready to go on, then you are in the right place. If you feel that you are being pushed along into something that is beyond your control and it is making you afraid, then you are in the right place. If you are uncertain why you are here, but find that you are irresistibly drawn back again and again, then you are in the right place.

Meditation

Start the 7D meditation by briefly running through the 5D meditations and then the 6D meditation. Picture or feel yourself as having arrived here in time and space from everywhere else. Feel the connectedness of yourself as a focal point for consciousness. Believe that you are newly born and like any new born baby are being held and cared for by loving parents. Allow this transition to take place.

At first you may feel vulnerable, but this will quickly pass. Gently float in the white light that now surrounds you. Feel your cares and worries being washed away and being replaced by bliss and serenity. Know that you have brought with you all that you need to survive and prosper. These things and abilities will be available to you as you need them. Know that you will attract to you the right people and circumstances to best help you to make this transition. Feel the tension in your neck and face relax. Believe that you are being rejuvenated from the inside out. Others will begin to comment on the fact that you are getting noticeable younger all of the time. Let go of emotional and physical pain. Let the loving energies heal you, believe that they can. See the beauty of yourself as you arrive here. Feel the completeness of your physical body as the light shines out from you into the 3D universe, sweeping all of the previous cares away with it. See and feel your oneness with an infinite universal intelligence that loves you more than you can imagine. Believe that this is your destiny. That this is exactly the way it is meant to be.

CHAPTER 38
SEVENTH DIMENSIONAL MEDITATIONS (CONT.)

The Seventh dimension is a marvelous piece of work. As a physical form it is perfect in every way. Your 7D body exists in the same place as your 3D body and includes it as part of its existence. Without manifesting through your 3D body, it is no longer the 7D. The Seventh dimension means seven separate dimensions merged together. If we subtract the three dimensions represented by the 3D, this leaves us with just four dimensions which comprise the 4D.

What we are attempting is both very complicated and very simple. It is only complicated when viewed from the 3D. It is very simple when viewed from the potential 7D. The potential 7D is the Seventh dimension without full realization. This is an interim state of being in the early levels of the 7D. Your Future Self is holding the structure of your 7D body in its mind. This is not easy for it because of your doubts and fears trying to pull it apart.

As you begin to exchange more fully with your future self you will become more and more responsible for your actions. Either this effort will become the most important focus for you, or your future self will pass on this life time and try again perhaps next life time if things go right. This is not a threat. A substantial number of lifetimes will be involved before you are through. Somewhere along the line it will happen, and that will be your last life time as you have come to know it. You will fully metamorphose into the next stage of consciousness while maintaining your physical form. This is as important to your future self as being born is to you.

Although very difficult, you can go a long way in this life time just by cleaning up past negative karma and not creating any new. Making a viable connection with your future self will carry through into the next life time. No one can predict the exact moment of your Seventh dimensional rebirth, but it will happen. We are like a baby in the womb. We cannot go back nor can we stay where we are. We may not like what is in store for us, we may think it unkind to be so rudely awakened, but like it or not we will be born.

Chapter 39
Seventh Dimensional Changes

You have reached a point where you may be experiencing great joy and enlightenment, but most likely you feel like a specimen pinned on a board. There is a point early in the 7D levels where you are severely tested, the way you might test a new race car. Your emerging self from the future wants to make sure you are emotionally ready to carry the increased spiritual power that comes with the mergence. The tests will come in various forms. When they are over, you will realize that you were being tested. You will also know if you passed or not. Don't worry, if you fail a test you will learn from it and prepare for the next test.

The 3D part of us wants to be something different from what it has always been. It wants to be able to do something spectacular or to have a God like flash of understanding. It wants to feel something *different*. When it doesn't seem to experience any of these things it gets discouraged and loses interest. It is necessary, in order to continue, to neutralize the last vestiges of self-centeredness and the need to be in control by completely surrendering to a power greater than our self. If we are unable to do this, then it is an indication that we are not ready in this life time to transcend our earth bound lessons.

The 3D you has a quality that is invisible to it. That quality is the ability *not* to realize it is changing. We are capable of great change while not realizing it. We are usually the last one to know. Usually friends or family members will tell us that we have changed before we realize that we have.

We have a quality that will always be with us. It is the ability to realize and accept any changes in us or in our environment as the new norm. We quickly adjust to the new levels and consider them as normal. This is a good quality. It allows us to experience tremendous change without harming our mental and emotional being. Adapting to change has allowed the human race to survive. The only problem with having this ability is if we are looking at temporary changes as a means of permanent satisfaction.

For example, let us say that you buy a new car. You are most likely going to be excited about it and wash it and keep it out of the Sun. But then something happens. Somewhere along the line it stops being a new car and simply becomes *your* car.

Know that you *are* changing. Part of that change is a continuous giving up of your sovereignty to a greater Self to form a new level of sovereignty that in turn needs to be transcended. A constant and ever faster process of acceptance and release. This is the very thing that allows you to grow. For us, this is an attribute that must continue forever. No matter how wonderful or powerful we may become, we will always be merging into something greater than ourselves, constantly realizing our unlimited potential.

With regards to spiritual growth, we are known by our "resistance". What this means is the more resistance we have to the change required by our Time Traveling Oversoul, the less evolved we seem. The more ego centric we are the less we are able to change. For example, let us say that you have a dog who, as you open the front door, knocks you down and runs away. You would, of course, consider this animal unevolved as compared to a dog who greeted you with your slippers. To our Time Traveling Oversoul, we are much like a pet. Consider that your Time Traveling Oversoul is many thousands of years older than you. Your entire lifetime is like a single day to it. If you present a problem by refusing to change, it can simply wait until tomorrow when it will try again.

If we are full of self and opinions about everything, if we are steadfastly routed behind a barricade of ego and self centeredness, then we will make little progress until we can realize that we are our own worst enemy. How can the Oversoul hope to bring about the drastic kinds of change necessary to bring you into a position where you can merge and interact without causing harm to either you or your environment?

There has to be some kind of organized regimen occurring from lifetime to lifetime from which your Soul—under the guidance of its Oversoul—can learn to influence you enough to get your attention. More importantly, is your willingness to look for and accept such a regimen. The necessity to turn your will over to a power greater than yourself is absolutely fundamental. It is then 7D changes can begin to happen.

Chapter 40

Introduction to the Eighth Dimension

Notice that from the Sixth dimension, we observe the Seventh dimension as a place of white light that exists within us. The juxtaposition of black and white is familiar to us from our earlier studies of the primordial universe where black and white polarization also existed. The difference is that the primordial universe was one-dimensional because our viewpoints were not able to grasp the multi-verse within them.

We have come full circle back to where we started, but like the prodigal son, we are much wiser for the journey. Another difference is that in the primordial universe the white and black universes were a result of polarization and as such could never be in the same place at the same time from our viewpoint. Now we have an expanded viewpoint that allows the white universe to exist within the black universe simultaneously. We have called these places dimensions because as we added each facet it has allowed an additional dimensional window that increased our consciousness and abilities.

We have learned and observed that because time is an illusion, we can experience separate instances in time coincidentally. We have also seen that the dimensions exist simultaneously as well. The Tenth dimension exists as a composite dimension comprised of its nine component parts that gestalt into the tenth. We have looked at seven of these parts. The remaining two parts are the Eight and Ninth dimensions. That these two dimensions exist within our grasp, but just outside of our normal consciousness, is a necessary realization for us. Without this realization we would never think to look for them.

You may be wondering how all of these dimensions could exist without anyone knowing about them? The answer is that they have been known about for many thousands of years. Highly advanced knowledge such as contained in these Chapters was considered sacred and was handed down by various priesthoods from generation to generation. It was felt that the general world consciousness was not ready to learn about these things and the knowledge was preserved for a time when it would be ready. Occasionally the line was broken and the knowledge would be lost for a time until it could be revived again by independent clairvoyant researchers. In our present time, the knowledge had been lost or deformed for a considerable time.

It might be easier for you to think of dimensions as accumulated viewpoints rather than dimensions. As an example, think of how the world would look if you observed it with only one eye. It would no longer look 3D because we would need two eyes to allow a 3D perspective. Now imagine how it might look with three eyes? Or four or ten? Rather than external eyes or viewpoints, we have—in addition to our two eyes—many more viewpoints available to us internally. We will examine a total of twelve of these viewpoints or dimensions as we progress in our studies, and a hint of the thirteenth.

The nature of the Eight dimension is the same as the nature of the Second and the Fifth dimensions, and is in fact just a more complete and inclusive extension of these. The 8D allows us access to a much more complete and open ended Self than has been previously available for us in the 3D. The 8D brings with it all of the potential of what is thought of as being Christ Conscious. When you fully experience the 8D you will know exactly who you are and why you are here. You bring with you an ever expanding knowledge of your perfect self. The 8d also brings with it an overwhelming capacity for love.

The 7D may have seemed disappointingly flat and 6D-like. This is for a necessary reason. As has been stated in earlier Chapters, the bliss levels of the 7D is the quality of love. It is not until we radiate out this bliss to others in the 8D that we can call it love. As we begin to experience love the 8D will begin to activate. This experience is the one you have been looking for. It brings forth from you a golden glow.

We have reached very subtle levels of realization. These levels have always existed within us, but we were not able to access them because we didn't know how. We must remember that even desiring these more subtle levels will keep them out of our reach. Also, we cannot attempt to hang on to them either for that will also push them away. They will only come to us as a natural result of the mergence with our Self from the future.

In the beginning you may only have small momentary glimpses of the 8D. This is a wonderful sign. Be patient and know that it is close. If this is meant to happen for you then it will happen. Nothing can stop it.

In the next Chapter we will take a look at the Ninth Dimension.

Chapter 41

Introduction to the Ninth Dimension

The Ninth dimension is the top of the 10D power structure. The 9D functions through the 6D into the 3D as the ability to do or accomplish. It is the creative force that has brought forth all that is created by man.

If you remember from earlier Chapters, the 3D imbues the first and second dimensions with the ability to have motion and 3D time. The 6D provides a protective barrier against degenerating back into the lesser dimensions. The 9D allows us to safely manifest our creative will directly into the physical dimensions without losing integrity. What this means in terms of power is very subtle and needs to be understood before we can proceed.

We generally think of power as some overwhelming force such as one person's dominance over another or a stronger country having power over a weaker neighbor. We think of power in terms of political clout or monetary leverage. These are 3D interpretations and have little to do with true power.

The kind of power that emanates from the Ninth dimension is without opposition and therefore absolute. 3D power depends upon opposition, a polarity of strong verses weak. 9D power stands alone and simply is. A person running 9D power brings into being whatever he/she wishes. The only opposition is in the form of resistance due to 3D time. In other words there is a time lag between the 9D visualization and the 3D manifestation.

A simple comparison of 3D power and 9D power can be seen in the following example. Suppose a person using 3D power suddenly realizes they have barely enough time to make an appointment across town. They rush to the car and rush to the highway only to discover bumper to bumper traffic. They change from lane to lane trying to make traffic lights. A feeling of frustration comes over them as they realize they are going to be late. Nothing they can do will get them there on time. It seems as though everything is working against them.

Now let us look at a person using 9D power, using the same scenario. They enter the same traffic to find a bumper to bumper condition, but rather than getting upset about it they envision arriving at the appointment on time. The congested traffic does not bother them because it is simply not a problem to them. They ignore the obvious problems and *know* that they will be on time. They are not the least bit concerned. Gradually traffic speeds up, the traffic lights are more green than red and our 9D person arrives at the appointment exactly on time.

The 3D person was concerned with overcoming opposition while the 9D person was without opposition. The 3D person was frustrated with the mounting barriers to his success while the 9D person was confident of success and unconcerned with barriers.

Of course there is a lot more to mastering 9D power and this will be covered in later Chapters. For now we are only being introduced to the 7th, 8th and 9th dimensions. The next Chapter will introduce you to the 10th dimension. It is from the 10D that we can safely learn to use the unlimited potentials found in all of its component dimensions.

CHAPTER 42

INTRODUCTION TO THE TENTH DIMENSION

The Tenth Dimension is a safe plateau from where we can begin to learn about our newly found powers. It is also the first true level of God consciousness.

It has been necessary to lightly touch on the 7th, 8th and 9th dimensions because they must be utilized in tandem from the 10D for which they were created. The main reason for bringing these dimensions up slowly and together is to bypass the inherent traps contained in each. Each trap can (and usually does) consume many lifetimes. As Time Travelers we have the luxury of knowing future lessons because we have experienced them all many times before. Our problem then lies in bringing this knowledge into our current *physical* body which has only existed in our past until now.

Reading a book on a subject does not make us an expert. Obviously reading a book about mountain climbing is not the same as actually climbing a mountain. We can intellectually grasp the concept of Tenth dimensional Being through study and meditation, but to live and operate as a Tenth dimensional Being takes devoted practice. By observing our feelings, actions and problems in everyday life we can pinpoint where we must concentrate our remedial studies.

Problems concerning human emotions and intellectual misconceptions are contained below the 6D. If you have problems with emotional issues such as hate, anger, procrastination, fear, etc..., methods for working through these are contained in the Chapters and Meditations that lead to the 6D. It is here that you will also find reasons and explanations to the whys and hows involved in attainment of Tenth dimensional Consciousness. The Sixth dimension is the result of neutralizing these feelings. By the time you reach the 6D you must be devoid of such common emotions, looking for neither highs or lows nor emotional cause and effect. Absolute detachment is necessary to proceed to the discovery of the true 7D. In Buddhism for example, bliss, wisdom and enlightenment of the 7D are the supreme goal. As Time Travelers we are seeking to discover additional dimensional facets beyond the 7D while including all that the 7D has to offer.

We can better understand the 7D by a quick study of the teachings of Gautama Buddha, but not to be lost in the morass of interpretation. We can learn from his advocation of dispassionate discernment leading to emotional detachment, leading to the transcendence of suffering and unsatisfactoriness. With the absence of base emotions—as the cause of these problems—comes wisdom, enlightenment and finally release.

We can likewise better understand the 8D by a quick study of the teachings of Jesus Christ, but also not to be lost in the morass of interpretation. His advocating of the golden rule to "do unto others as you would have them do unto you", and that we should love one another. These are both simple yet astoundingly powerful recommendations.

We can also better understand the 9D by a quick study of the dialog between Krishna and Arjuna in the Bhagavad-gita. In it are contained the keys to universal power through the detachment from illusion.

For hints about the 10D we can look to the Koran and the teachings of Mohammed.

I am sure that there are many persons and teachings that exemplify each dimension. I have selected the above because I know them to be examples representing a respective dimension in some way.

Our job is to extract the essence from the teachings of each of these great men, and then to blend them into something that is a combination of each of them but is not any one of them. Such is the nature of God Consciousness.

The Tenth dimension gives us access to the Third dimension in a way that has only been dreamed of in this time period. It opens the possibilities of "Heaven on Earth". However, we have so far only touched upon the Tenth dimension intellectually. Lest we forget, the Tenth dimension is comprised of nine complete and uniquely separate dimensions all operating independently to form the completed 10D.

As a newly forming tenth dimensional center we are like the new born baby gazing beatifically at all that surrounds it, eyes wide with wonder.

Even from such an exalted dimension as the 10D, it is well to remember that the true self contained in the Eleventh dimension has not yet arrived. Like a dutiful servant we are still preparing the vessel in which the approaching self will dwell while it quietly oversees the operation unseen from outside of our knowledge. We have much work to do in the brief moment we are physically alive. It is good to prioritize what is important to us. Whether it is the blatancy of the obvious world around us, temporary and nagging, or the gossamer promises of a permanent world as yet unseen by us.

CHAPTER 43

TENTH DIMENSIONAL CLARIFICATIONS

This and the next several Chapters will attempt to clarify what we have so far studied and begin to focus on our immediate group goals and possibilities.

The physical dimensions are seemingly so much more concrete and demanding than the extended dimensions. This has a tendency to short-circuit our attention and energies much like a toothache detracts from the joys of a piece of chocolate. The everyday demands are so overwhelming that we are lucky to make time for ourselves, let alone find time to discover new dimensions. After a busy day we have a tend to party (if we are younger) or we turn on the T.V., or enjoy our family (unless we are in the middle of a divorce), or we read or sleep, or surf the net, etc...

A few of us look for something beyond the obvious. Some of us find some of what we are looking for in various religions. Some of us delve into exotic philosophies and mystical books. We try meditations, gurus, magic pills and magic spells. We find that somehow we are not satisfied with what is being handed to us as "the truth". We believe with an ever increasing hunger that there must be more.

A Course In Time Travel is an attempt at bringing as many options as possible into as clear a focus as possible. Because this course was interpreted and written by a human being it means that it is fallible, but it is at least a start in breaking the patterns that invisibly enslave us. I look to future students of this work to fine tune the interpretations and to better explain the subtleties involved. There is nothing as successful as success, meaning that as some of you begin to find the hidden beauty behind the words, you can share your successes with others, further refining and validating this endeavor.

I have maintained that I am just like you in that I am no one special. My gift has been one of exceptional clairvoyance and dogged persever-ance over a long period of time and an unwavering need to pierce the veil. I am aware that most of you are not able to devote the amount of time and concentration needed to solve the puzzle that is at the heart of Time Travelers. I have sought to solve the puzzle for myself and share what I have found with you. I am happy within myself that I have come a long way in doing so and am immeasurably the better for it.

Whether or not we are successful does not matter in the short run. What is important is that the concepts have been imported into this time period and into the earth's "Akashic Records." The work we do now might not be fully understood and incorporated until a thousand years in our future. This is perfectly acceptable in view of the uncounted eons of entrapment and mass misunderstanding we have already endured.

We are passing through perhaps the most exciting time in our existence. A time of overwhelming discovery and possibility. A time when the outer consciousness merged with the inner to produce unimaginable beauty. I am honored to be some small part of this.

Chapter 44
Opportunities

Human thought seems to manifest in quantum leaps. A period of time transpires where little or no original thought occurs. Then, for no apparent reason, tremendous progress in thought begins to happen. It might come from a single individual or a group or groups. It might come through a single source such as music or science or through a broad spectrum of disciplines. Then just as suddenly as it started it ends.

As Time Travelers we are participating in the beginning of one of these quantum leaps. If we can fully grasp the meaning of this surge of understanding we—like surfers on an endless wave—will have the potential to forever be on the leading edge of new thought. This is an amazingly exciting potential, and one I would loath to miss. To be a part of such a golden opportunity, no amount of effort would be too much. Such opportunities are rare and must be seized with both hands.

How many times has opportunity knocked on your door only to find you unwilling to take advantage of it? A fact that you later regretted? Life has a way of quickly passing. By the time we understand this it is too late. It is a sad fact that the average person in this time period had little chance of awakening. We existed in a catatonic morass of habits and routines. We needed to be constantly entertained lest we go mad from boredom. We exalted those who successfully entertained us and punished those who tried but failed.

Chapter 45

Tenth Dimensional Clarifications (Cont.)

The Tenth dimension is a complex consisting of ten separate dimensions all working together. Since we have learned not to differentiate or discriminate between the lower five dimensions, having resolved them into a single working entity, as viewed and operated from the void of the Sixth dimension, we are left with the extended dimensions which resolve into the Thirteenth dimension.

I wish to take a moment here to clarify what we are looking at. With so many additional dimensions looming on the horizon, it may seem a bit overwhelming, but let me assure you that once understood, it will all resolve into an easily understandable singularity.

It is important to know that the sixth dimension is the center of two mirror universes. There are six internal dimensions which exist in much higher rates of vibration and six external dimensions we have been studying. Understand that these mirror universes are polar opposites which resolve back into six extended dimensions which we will call the seventh through the twelfth. It is in this resolved configuration that the seventh dimension becomes the new 3D physical body.

The seventh dimensional body[1], which represents the physical body of your inner being, is able to interface with the third dimension with clarity, power and enlightenment, depending upon the quality of the work you have done up to this point. Realize that the light of the 7D has always shone brightly from within you. Whether it is able to penetrate the dross of your lower dimensional bodies depends entirely upon the work you are doing now.

It has been stated that the 10D is the first level of a physical complex consisting of the 10D, 11D and the 12D, which resolves into the 13D. This complex of the 13D will take you beyond the bounds of self into what is called the *Collective Consciousness*. It is here that you will be able to realize combined multiple realities and dimensions in such a way that you exist in a completely new and different three-dimensional reality from the one in which you are now trapped. All future and past events coincide which transcends time as we know it

---

[1] The *Stellar* body.

three-dimensionally.

From the 13D it is impossible to experience reality other than in absolute perfection in its myriad forms. It is here that the omniscience, omnipotence and omnipresent of God consciousness, and the quality of undiluted Christ consciousness, are essential basics for each participating individual. Each individual enjoys complete sovereignty and yet is an integral working part of the infinite whole.

A Word About the 13D

So completely different is existence here that it cannot be recognized as having once been the 3D. The 3D you now reside in still remains intact just as you see it now. Changes here are done through the 7th, 8th and 9th dimensions. They are temporary and affect only your immediate surroundings.

Because in the 13D we experience all possible time and realities at the same time, we are no longer involved with individual realities or individual time tracks and events. This means that the reality you enjoy today will still continue with you in it, but it will become a single minute part of your complete reality unnoticed by the new perspective you have as the 13D self. This relationship exists as a universal *now* outside of the time and space we normally refer to as the "here and now". The difference is one of changing view points to include and merge with the 13D from our perspective, and to extend the influence of the 13D as far as possible into the physical dimensions.

Each isolated consciousness in each individual reality, anywhere in time, is capable of eventually transcending itself by merging into the "Greater Reality". The intent of the Greater Reality is to push into all of its sub-realities, no matter how insignificant or remote they may be, in order to gradually bring them into *The Collective*.

From the viewpoint of *The Collective*, all of these many dimensions that may seem so strange to us have been mastered by it. It is only these lower dimensions that we are familiar with that need to be mastered by it to complete its agenda. This puts us in a very good position to rapidly expand our consciousness beyond anything we might have imagined. Exactly how fast this will occur will be different for each of us because the law of "free will" is still the lowest common denominator.

The 13D is a perfect combination of all other dimensions and possibilities, existing on top of and because of them. It contains the best of Heaven and Hell.

CHAPTER 46
NINTH DIMENSIONAL POWER

As power is concerned, in our 3D reality we as Time Travelers are faced with having to walk a very narrow path. If we stray even momentarily we reap instant karma. Since our intent is usually for the greatest good, our karma is usually bad coming into cause and effect with pre-existing out of balance conditions. On the other hand, if we make no choices, we still find ourselves in unenviable positions. We see ruthless people wallowing in opulence while often times we who have worked hard for spiritual enlightenment and being hobbled with moral constraints, can barely eke out an existence. The question is, how can we function here without getting kicked around by our environment? The answer is the passive power that is found in the 9D.

With a little practice the following techniques can be mastered and can actually be a lot of fun. Passive power is about having choices. It is about selecting which reality you will experience from existing possibilities. As an example, when you fill your plate from a buffet you make choices from what is available. Karmically it does not matter which selections you make. It would matter if you selected something that was not available. It might disappoint or embarrass you. You could wind up with no food at all even though you paid for it.

Many of us go through life in this way, making disappointing choices that were not available to start with. In other words, our expectations exceed our immediate possibilities, and we are usually not aware that we have sabotaged ourselves before we even got started. We are not aware that our failures are a direct result of not knowing what our choices were.

9D techniques allow you to know exactly what choices are available and how to select the best one for you. This works very much like selecting a station on the radio. You might flip from one station to another until you find one that you like. You might be looking for Classical but find that this choice is not available, so you settle for New Age instead. You picked the best choice for you from the possibilities that are available. In our 3D world most people believe that the first choice they are given is the *only* choice available. They want Classical but wind up with 24 hour weather reports. They are unaware that they have choices.

Making choices has nothing to do with being selfish or not being selfish. It has nothing to do with whether you deserve your choice or not. It is just a mechanical selection of either this or that. You make a conscious choice of whether to step on the nail or not to step on the nail.

The technique I will share with you in this Chapter is called *Changing Channels*.

Changing Channels

Changing Channels can be implemented in several ways, however certain rules must be observed:

1. Do *not* to accept the first choice given to you unless it is one you want.

2. Make a choice that is available.

3. Do not to accept a choice you do not want unless there is no better choice.

4. Once you have made a choice, claim it as your own.

It is important to become as emotionally unattached to your decision as possible. Be neither for or against. The more emotion that enters into your choice, the more limited your choices become.

Changing Channels is very effective in thwarting an argument. By going emotionally neutral the words from the other person fall upon the ground. They will stop immediately. In these cases you do not even need to say anything.

You can start Changing Channels on little things that do not matter. The trick is to do it without the other person realizing that you are doing anything. As you progress you can begin to affect larger areas of your reality.

CHAPTER 47

EIGHT DIMENSIONAL CLARIFICATIONS

In this Chapter we will be discussing the 8D in relation to the part it plays as an integral part of the 10D. The Eighth dimension is the seat of consciousness for the Tenth dimension. In and by itself, the 8D is technically Christ consciousness, although the 10D is the first physical level of God consciousness. The 8D is the center of awareness for the 10D in the same way that the 11D is the center of awareness for the 13D.

The basic difference between the Eighth and Eleventh dimensions is monumental. The 11D is a potentially infinite multiplication of the 8D. Where the 8D is the apex of perfect expanding individual realization, the 11D is the transcendence of the self as an individual, and begins the incorporation of the Collective Consciousness as the self.

The Tenth dimension serves a dual function:

1. It is a complete vehicle, with its physical vehicle based in the 7D as the *Stellar Body*. Its centralized consciousness is housed in the 8D, and its power structure accessible from the 9D.

2. It serves as the physical vehicle for the Thirteenth dimension.

If you recall from earlier Chapters, the 7D relates to the Between the Eyes Center. It is a place of white light and single-pointedness. The 8D relates to the Crown Center which has access to the billion or so cells of the brain which represents the Milky way. It is easy to see the differences between the two. Where the 7D establishes the consciousness of a single star, the 10D establishes the consciousness of a galaxy. By the same token, the 13D establishes the consciousness of all Galaxies. There are expanded consciousness far beyond even this, but it would not serve us to discuss them at this time.

The Eight dimensional consciousness places us in the precarious position of having unlimited powers of understanding and feeling, but without the active power to create our realities. This will come with the mastery of the greater dimensions to come. Meanwhile, we must still take our directions from our Eleventh dimensional self. It has the knowledge of where you fit into the scheme of planetary consciousness. You have reached a point that you can do more harm than good by forcing 12D realities without 11D understanding. We have examples of this in the politics of this time period. They are like puppies on a karmic freeway.

As discussed in the previous Chapter, we have limited passive power to choose from existing possibilities in our realities. It is important *not* to initiate new realities because of unnecessary karma which may slow down your progress. We must take our guidance from that part of ourselves that knows what to create and when to create it. This ability comes from beyond intellectual capabilities. It is an integral part of the functioning of your future self. In other words, you are still forming. The real you is still on the way.

Although tempting, it is better to wait for yourself to arrive before using your new powers. Using the 9D is perfectly fine. However, because of its integral connection with the power structure of the 12D, some of us might figure out how to use the unlimited power of the 12D to our detriment. If you are patient at this juncture, you will progress much faster. You are in a delicate phase of unfoldment. If you take charge prematurely, you can derail yourself, and possibly even forestall the merger with your Time Traveling Oversoul.

I would suggest reviewing these Chapters. Each time you read them, new meaning and understanding will be given to you, especially as each new Chapter is revealed.

CHAPTER 48

DETAILED EXAMINATION OF CONSCIOUSNESS (REVIEW)

What is the difference between God, Christ, Cosmic, Buddhic and Krishnic consciousness?

I have taken the liberty of repeating Chapters 18-21 as a review of the nature and structure of consciousness. The reason I have included this review in these last few Chapters is twofold:

1. I believe this material to be so fundamental to understanding and transcending current limitations in consciousness, that it needs to be amplified.

2. The material contained in this review might be more easily understood and retained after having studied the interim Chapters 23-47.

The definitions contained in this Chapter and those that follow in this series supersede all other definitions contained in this course. By this I mean if a contradiction occurs in the definitions found in earlier Chapters and those now being presented, defer to the later Chapters. The reason for this is because a more exacting examination of consciousness produces a more exact definition and understanding of the underlying mystery.

Consider our earlier examination of primordial consciousness when we saw that the void contained a substance called ether with the potential which was capable of producing all that we experience today. We further saw that this substance was subject to continuous inherent vibration which produced polar opposites. At one pole was the Void which was devoid of all motion. At the other pole was maximum vibration which produced White Light.

The nature of vibration dictates that there is a stair step process of going from the Void to White Light and back again to the Void. Each of these four states[1] is the beginning of a different kind of consciousness.

---

[1] The Void, White Light, going from the Void to White Light and going from White Light to the Void.

The Void is the birthplace of what the ancients termed Sagittarius which in its most extended state is called Cosmic consciousness. This is also the beginning of what we call the Fourth dimension and all that we call spiritual.

The White Light state is the birthplace of what the ancients called Leo which is the beginning of Christ consciousness, and what we call the Fifth dimension.

Ascending vibration upon the ether from the Void to the White Light state is called Buddhic consciousness, while descending vibration upon the ether coming from the White Light state to the Void is called Krishnic consciousness. The action of going from the Void towards White Light is part of the nature of Sagittarius.

The action of going from White Light towards the Void is part of the nature of what the ancients called Aries. Aries is the birthplace of what we call the Third dimension.

First let us examine in detail the White Light state called the Christ. The White Light state shown is static in that it is without motion by virtue of magnetic attraction. We have seen this state before as the goal of Buddhic consciousness. In that context it is called Nirvana. It is called Heaven in the western world. What is found here is called bliss or ecstasy when compared to any other state of being.

It is interesting to note that the Christ in this primal state has not the ability to exhibit love. This ability which is so characteristic of Christ consciousness does not appear until we experience it in its subdivided descent into duality. There is instead universal compassion which is characteristic of Buddhic consciousness. Also note the Christ at this level is composed of all other potential consciousness except for God consciousness which is a polar opposite of Christ consciousness and at the same time contains it.

We can see from *Figure 48.1* that all other consciousness are derived from the Christ. It is for this reason that many think that the Christ is in fact God. We can understand why many would also believe in this state of being as the ultimate goal for humanity.

It is important to remind ourselves that those who seek God consciousness have chosen a much more difficult course of action than those who seek to simply return to the Christ. This is not to deride the latter for the choice is up to the individual. However please note the direction of creative intent from the Christ. This would suggest that those who simply seek refuge in the Christ will at some time feel

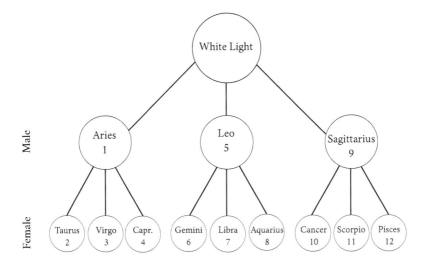

Figure 48.1: God Consciousness

the urge to re-descend into matter.

In the next Chapter we will continue to examine these four types of consciousness.

CHAPTER 49

DETAILED EXAMINATION OF CONSCIOUSNESS
(CONT.)

We learned in the previous Chapter that the primordial positive pole is also the primordial Christ. We also learned that this same place is called Nirvana by some and Highest Heaven by others. This is an astoundingly important piece of information and one most metaphysical researchers have missed. This is the place that Adam and Eve (primordial man and woman) "fell" from. Or were they pushed by an inherent creative urge to manifest into the planes of duality and the third dimension?

I was asked by a Time Traveler member if, upon the return to the Christ, it would be permanent. Would one then exist in this exalted state in ever lasting life? I don't know. It certainly has all of the elements for permanence although we can all attest that it is possible for us to "fall" from this august place as well. It probably depends upon the individual as to whether the return is permanent or not. I personally believe that Christ consciousness is an interim step to God consciousness.

Remember that there are two major paths. One is the Angelic path, having Heaven and existence within the Christ as the goal. The other is the God path with a continuing participation in creation and never-ending unfoldment of God consciousness as the goal. Of the two, Heaven is obviously a much easier and finite goal to reach through the regimented Angelic hierarchy. God consciousness on the other hand is open-ended. It is a never-ending accumulation of knowledge and power in addition to all that the Christ principle has to offer. God consciousness, being all-inclusive, includes all that the Christ is without being confined by it.

As we recall, the Christ principle is all that is internal in God consciousness and can be thought of as the personality—or quality—of God. God consciousness on the other hand is both all that is external (quantity) *and* all that is internal.

It is good to remember that the basic difference between God consciousness and Christ consciousness is one of placement and perspective. In God consciousness, the Christ is the internalized quality of the self whereas in Christ consciousness, God exists as an externalized parent.

DETAILED EXAMINATION OF CONSCIOUSNESS: BUDDHIC CONSCIOUSNESS

Review

We have seen in previous Chapters that vibration acting upon a substance called the "Ether"—or Einstein's "fabric of space"—causes a polarization, a condition of opposites. One pole is pure energy without motion. The other pole is this same pure energy in a state of maximum vibration or motion.

Because the negative pole—or Void—appears to be first in order, it is called the First dimension. The other pole, because of its relationship to the First pole, becomes a second dimension which is contained by the first. Because of this duality we call it the Second dimension.

Please note that the Second dimension is *contained* by the First dimension. This means that the Primordial 2D as a polar opposite is contained in the center or inside of (be it infinite or finite) the Primordial 1D. This is important because it sets the precedence for unipolar construction.

If you will examine this place with me, you will see that the primordial 2D is a place of endless White Light without any distinguishing features. Although we have identified it as the primordial Christ, it is static and without love due to it being completely self-contained. It exists in a pure state of "Self" without any concept of there being anything outside of itself. The lack of reflected replicated selves removes the characteristic magnetic attraction that would normally identify this as a place or property of what is loosely termed the Christ Principle.

Upon closer examination, this place is everything we identify as Nirvana and as being the apex of Buddhic consciousness. While this may seem strange and paradoxical at first, it is completely understandable given the fact that *all* facets of consciousness and created form are derived from the same primordial substance. The myriad differences which arrive from this cosmic womb are all simply unique combinations of the original. Knowing this takes much of the mystery out of the equation, but after all this is what we are attempting to accomplish isn't it?[1]

The above brings up an interesting point. If the Primordial 2D is the original Christ, then how could it also be Nirvana or Buddhic consciousness? Does this mean that they are the same? They are in a sense the same, but in a larger and more fundamentally important sense, they are completely different. It is this difference that we will now examine.

Stated as simply as possible, Christ consciousness exhibits a condition of permanence when achieved as a result of the *accumulation* and *centralization* of consciousness while achieving complete detachment from the separate constituent parts and levels of consciousness within *itself*. In other words, Christ consciousness is a completeness beyond the accumulated parts, but is always experienced from *within* the nature of this consciousness as internal beingness or Divine Self, which we call the Christ Principle.

When we contrast the above with Buddhic consciousness we find we are dealing with the same place and the same nature of consciousness, but from the *outside*. Furthermore and most importantly, Buddhic consciousness is achieved through detachment and not the accumulation of the separate constituent parts and levels of consciousness found within the Christ Principle.

The accumulation is inadvertent because of upward vibratory motion through the structure of consciousness within a human being. Consequently, it ultimately becomes subjected to a self-induced state of simulated nonexistence so devastating that it forces a simultaneous and inadvertent accumulation of the separate constituent parts and levels of consciousness within form, called the *Sagittarius Principle*. It is then that a temporary state of white light and Primordial Christ consciousness is subsequently experienced. This achievement is *temporary* because of the forward motion that has been set into effect in achieving it, a result of the nature and methods used to achieve Buddhic consciousness. It is this temporariness and non-centralized consciousness that is characteristic of Buddhic consciousness.

---

[1] Remember that the Primordial White Light state "exists" in our "now" and in our "space", and is accessible within our being at any time via the correct combination of viewpoints.

DETAILED EXAMINATION OF CONSCIOUSNESS: KRISHNIC CONSCIOUSNESS

Review

In the last several Chapters, we have looked at the primordial structure of each kind of consciousness. Now we will look at Krishnic consciousness and then proceed on to God consciousness.

Krishnic consciousness was so named after its chief practitioner Lord Krishna, best known to us from the Bhagavad-Gita[1]. This part of consciousness represents the return from White Light back to the material planes or 3D.

The major distinguishing characteristic of Krishnic consciousness is that of a continual selfless giving, regardless of consequence. The practitioner finds himself descending from an exalted level of consciousness to lower levels of consciousness to help those less fortunate then himself. Unfortunately, there is an inadvertent reduction of vibration resulting in the practitioner arriving with the same level of consciousness as those he would help. We humorously call this the "Law of Punishment for the Good Samaritan".

We can identify it by the Time Traveler definitions as a coming from the light and going towards lower vibrations of the physical planes. This identifies it as belonging to the Aries principle. We know that Aries is the outward expansion of consciousness from the light (or Sun) to the Void. This includes all outward motion.

Its polarization, in relation to its twin sister Buddhic consciousness, is male. If you will recall, there are three major principles in creation regarding vibration and motion. We have labeled these:

1. Outward motion, or Aries

---

[1] Technically, Krishnic consciousness is said to be representative of Vishnu the preserver which represents both birth and death. Originally Vishnu represented the complete wheel of life and death which would include Buddhic consciousness as one half of the wheel. When I refer to Krishnic consciousness however, I am referring only to the descending masculine side of the wheel. The Buddhists refer to this consciousness as "Buddhas of Compassion".

2. Inward motion, or Sagittarius and

3. Stationary centralization, or Leo

We could say that all motion and conscious viewpoints under Aries are outward bound[2]. This is also our definition of the Third dimension. We could also say that all motion and conscious viewpoints under Sagittarius are inward bound[3]. This is also our definition of the Fourth dimension.

We could say that all indwelling or centralized and static consciousness and viewpoints[4] belong to Leo, the Christ principle. This is also our definition of the Fifth dimension.

Fibnally, we could say that all of the above principles belong to something we call *God consciousness*, which is a gestalt beyond all that we have studied.

God Consciousness

As has been stated previously in the *A Course in Time Travel*, our goal is the never-ending pursuit of God consciousness. It is never-ending because there is no end to the possibilities and levels of being that can be experienced. Here I quote from an earlier Chapter: "Mystics that have experienced some little of what is available have all been at a loss to even begin to express what they experienced. These "little touches" are so far beyond our everyday existence that it is impossible to communicate in words, and indeed in anything less than the experience itself, what it is like. We are reduced to terms like ineffable and consummate when trying to describe in words what these mystics have reported. It would be like trying to say to a blind person what the starry night looked like, or trying to verbalize to a child the delights of adulthood." .

As we have said, God consciousness is a perfectly balanced array of all other consciousness and viewpoints. Once achieved, this basic combined viewpoint can be enhanced as to quality, ability and understanding. This means that one can attain God consciousness and still appear very flat and uninteresting in the beginning levels.

---

[2] Doingness and physicality.

[3] Beingness and spirituality.

[4] Knowingness and self realization.

CHAPTER 52

DETAILED EXAMINATION OF CONSCIOUSNESS: CHRIST CONSCIOUSNESS

Review

Christ consciousness is characterized by a centralization of the self from which all expression emanates. The key element here is the position of the self within the Self. Its chief component is *Love*.

Lesser levels denote possessive love and self-centeredness. Often, an overriding desire to save the world is evident believing that they are the one and only true Christ returning to the world to reign for a thousand years. This is called the Messianic complex.

Lesser levels of this can be found in people whom we call "long suffering". They all revolve around an out-of-balance positive position. When pursued to extremes, some of these people are haunted by a paranoia of self-created consummate evil sometimes referred to as "demons" or the "AntiChrist". This is not to say that these manifestations are unreal. To those who suffer in this state of reality, these manifestations are terrifyingly real. They are however the product of a forced spiritual out-of-balance condition.

Although we know instinctively that there is something terribly wrong and out-of-balance when we see these conditions in others or in loved ones, it is almost impossible to know that there is something wrong when it is happening to us. In fact, it is quite the opposite. While in Christ consciousness, we perceive everyone else as being somehow infected with "evil", and they must "repent" in order to be like us.

More complete levels of Christ consciousness denote Universal Love, overwhelming feelings of compassion and bliss and a desperate need to share these feelings. While on the surface it is hard to fault universal love and compassion, especially in this spiritually dark Age we live in, it is nonetheless an out-of-balanced condition that results in a sort of divine paranoia within the practitioner. Specifically, it violates the "Law of Equality". This means that the Christ is always the central figure while adoring (and usually sickly) crowds of people surround him, basking in his light, further adding to the delusion.

To effectively help replicate greater levels of consciousness from higher potentials to lower potentials, it is necessary to maintain a strict level of equality. Otherwise there will be a strong tendency to inadvertently promote inequality. This is usually followed by the Deification of the Avatar/Teacher, further widening the gap in the potential for multidimensional consciousness, rather than promoting it. We must fervently avoid the tendency of "Man worshiping Man".

The Christ, as portrayed by Jesus, combined out-of-balance good and a polarization with what he perceived as "Satan" or the "Antichrist", making for a predictable potential for martyrdom as was purportedly witnessed two thousand years ago.

Necessity of experiencing Christ Consciousness

Let me be quick to add that at a point in spiritual development it is necessary to experience Christ consciousness and eventually transcend it. Those who have not the wherewithal to transcend it shall follow this lesson into the after life, to be repeated in subsequent incarnations, and this is how it should be.

Those of us who find that we no longer call ourselves "Christians" need not feel guilty or harbor a shadow of doubt that we are somehow the "Antichrist". All of the brainwashing that has resulted from this two thousand year old cult is designed to place doubt and fear into you for purposes of control. This was a good and necessary moral step for the church to take in that much simpler time when we as the people were also much simpler. Far from invalidating the lesson, you have simply out grown it and now it is time to go on the next lesson.

In the next Chapter we will examine Cosmic consciousness and compare it to Christ, Buddhic and Krishnic consciousness. We will begin to see how all of these component consciousness fit together to eventually form God consciousness.

CHAPTER 53

DETAILED EXAMINATION OF CONSCIOUSNESS: COSMIC CONSCIOUSNESS

Maurice Bucke wrote an interesting book by the title of *Cosmic Consciousness*. He claimed that man was undergoing an evolutionary leap to new levels of awareness as great as any in our history. But exactly what is Cosmic consciousness? If you surf the internet looking for definitions, you will find that people know about Cosmic consciousness and that it is something truly wonderful and different, but are unable to tell you exactly what it is and why it is different from other types of consciousness.

In this Chapter I will attempt to put together all of the information on this subject that we have studied in previous Chapters, adding some other ideas and interesting facts about it as well. We saw in the last Chapter that Christ consciousness was more associated with the centralized placement and confinement of consciousness.

Cosmic consciousness is associated with decentralization and unconfined space. We also defined Cosmic consciousness as being composed of the exact same number of components as Christ consciousness and being identically equal, but from a multidimensionally mirrored position. Equal in every way, but exactly opposite.

If you will remember from previous Chapters, I gave a brief list of definitions for the origins of consciousness. If you will permit me, I will list them here in review:

These definitions are summed up below:

1. The *Void* is the birthplace of what the ancients termed *Sagittarius* which—in its most evolved state—is called Cosmic consciousness. As a subdivision of God consciousness it is further subdivided into Buddhic and Krishnic consciousness. To achieve Cosmic consciousness, one must resolve Buddhic and Krishnic consciousness into one consciousness. This is done by transcending and blending them to gain access to the Void.

2. The *White Light* state is the birthplace of what the ancients called *Leo*, which is the beginning of Christ consciousness. There are

four major subdivisions of Christ consciousness, each denoting a distinct manifestation of constituent facets of the archetypal Universal Christ principle. However, as in Cosmic consciousness, Christ consciousness is also subdivided into two major components, namely Buddhic and Krishnic consciousness. Again, as in Cosmic consciousness, these two basic ingredients play a major role. In order to achieve Christ consciousness, one must resolve Buddhic and Krishnic consciousness into one consciousness. This is done by transcending and blending them to gain access to the *Light*, much in the same way Cosmic consciousness is obtained.

By the above definitions, we see that Cosmic consciousness was associated with Sagittarius. Sagittarius is the "Mother" principle, as compared to Aries as the "Father" principle, Leo being the Universal child or "Son" principle.

In earlier definitions, we said that the major difference between Christ and Cosmic consciousness was one of position. Where Christ consciousness is always *internalized*, Cosmic consciousness is always *externalized*. For example, in *Figure 53.1*, you can see that every Sign of the Zodiac comes under the heading of the Christ. Everything else is considered Cosmic consciousness. But what about everything else? It seems that everything is consumed by the Christ as component parts. How can there be something else when we have accounted for all of the parts? By understanding this question, we will solve one of the greatest mysteries in human consciousness—that of dichotomy[1].

Consider for a moment the idea of Christ consciousness as being internal, as opposed to Cosmic consciousness which is external. What does this mean exactly? How does this relate to our everyday existence? If we look to our physical bodies as examples, we know that we have a physical body and it has a centralized consciousness we call our "self". In addition to this, our body has the ability to move and experience "time".

From our previous studies you should be able to spot the Christ principle as being connected with the centralized consciousness. This is the part we consider as ourselves. We have a name, likes and dislikes,

---

[1] The existence of paradox in the form of diametrically opposed consciousness existing within us at the same time in the same place, made out of the same components, while being relatively unaware of one another.

memories of our past experiences and hopes and desires for the future. Furthermore, we reside in a physical body which enables us to move around and have physical contact with the outside world.

If the internal part of us represents the Christ principle, then by definition, everything else would have to be associated with the Cosmic principle. If you look closely at the juxtaposition of Christ and Cosmic principles, you will see several dichotomies which I have listed below:

1. We have the dichotomy or polarization of the Christ and Cosmic principles. These are, by previous definition, two halves of God consciousness.

2. We have the resolved dichotomy or polarization within the Cosmic principle. This resolved internal dichotomy leading to external unlimited realization is a main characteristic of Cosmic consciousness. We have seen this previously as a polarization of Buddhic and Krishnic consciousness, and again as a polarization of Sagittarius and Aries as principles. Here in the example of our body, the delineation is less clear cut, but is still a good and valid example. If you look carefully, you will see that what is left after we remove the Christ principle from our body, is the physical body itself, and its ability to move. If we can separate the physical body from its abilities, then, suddenly, we see the Cosmic dichotomy.

3. Universal Christ consciousness, once it is accessed, is full blown, perfect and complete. Nothing can be missing or it would no longer be Christ consciousness. Universal Cosmic consciousness, on the other hand, is made from myriad pieces and parts in an unending process of work and self discovery.

4. We have the unresolved external dichotomy or polarization with Cosmic consciousness, which is essential to the Christ principle. This unresolved external dichotomy is a main characteristic of Christ consciousness. In other words, Christ consciousness is consummately familiar with the light and not with the void.

If you will look at the diagram for a moment, I believe we can finalize the basic difference between Christ and Cosmic consciousness.

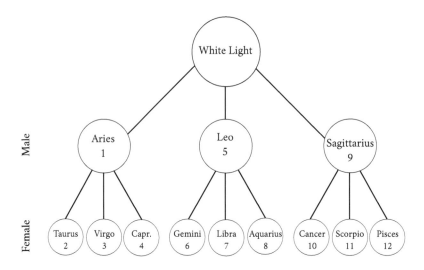

Figure 53.1: God Consciousness

Think of the white globe as the Sun. In our Solar System, the Sun is the Christ principle. The Planets represent individualized consciousness, which are separate from the Sun. The combined planetary consciousness represents the Cosmic Principle, but doesn't represent the entire Solar System. The God Principle would be a combination of the Sun and all of the planets. In other words, God consciousness is the *complete* Solar System, existing as something far greater than the sum of its parts.

Then what is so different and great about Cosmic consciousness? The reason it is as great but different as compared to Christ consciousness is that it provides a seamless cohesiveness to an infinite universe that is not found in Christ consciousness. It gives access to the cosmos through an ever-growing universal understanding that is both great in its diversity and in its ability to resolve that diversity into perfect unity, instantly finding order in the place of chaos. To better understand these two underlying components of God consciousness, is to better understand God consciousness, which we will examine in the nect Chapter.

CHAPTER 54

DETAILED EXAMINATION OF CONSCIOUSNESS: GOD CONSCIOUSNESS

Review

As has been stated previously, our goal is the never-ending pursuit of God consciousness. It is never-ending because there is no end to the possibilities and levels of Being that can be experienced. Mystics who have experienced some little of what is available have all been at a loss to even begin to express what happened to them. As we have said, God consciousness is a perfectly balanced array of all other consciousness and viewpoints. Once achieved, this basic combined viewpoint can be continually enhanced as to quality, ability and understanding.

How is God Consciousness Different from its Components?

In our final examination of consciousness in this series on the various kinds of consciousness, we will take a look at why God consciousness is superior to any other kind of consciousness, and summarize its distinguishing features.

As we have seen in the last few Chapters, there are four major components of God consciousness, namely Christ, Cosmic, Krishnic and Buddhic. We have seen how each is an integral part of God consciousness and how each differed from the other. Although we have seen many indications of what God consciousness is, in this Chapter we will gather together those qualities and definitions into one place for purposes of reference and further understanding.

Let us begin by listing the components of God consciousness.

Components of God Consciousness

1. Christ consciousness (See Chapter 18)

2. Cosmic consciousness (See Chapter 19)

3. Buddhic consciousness (See Chapter 20)

4. Krishnic consciousness (See Chapter 21)

In God consciousness, we see an interplay of all of these consciousness as being inseparable. This interplay and fusion of consciousness into a single entity that gestalts far beyond its individual components, is probably the most distinguishing feature of God consciousness. We have previously defined God consciousness as having the universal qualities of:

1. Omniscience—having total knowledge; knowing everything.

2. Omnipresence—being present everywhere simultaneously.

3. Omnipotence—having unlimited or universal power, authority, or force; all-powerful.

However, for the individual, the above qualities exist as potential that can never fully be reached. The reason for this is in the definition of the unlimited potential for us as individual beings in our pursuit of God consciousness.

In simpler terms, one of the most wonderful things about coming into God consciousness is the fact that we are finite beings expanding into unlimited potential. It seems then, that we, as finite beings, need a more specific set of definitions then has previously been given.

Specific Definitions for God Consciousness
(As Pertains to Human Beings)

1. Unattainable.

2. As having unlimited levels of realization.

3. And as being an on going process rather than something one attains all at once.

This means that no two persons who attain God consciousness will probably be at the exact same level of understanding and mastery at the same time. It also means that probably no two persons will process God consciousness at the same rates of realization.

How can a person come into the process of being "God conscious" and still function in the "real world"? As we approach the Thirteenth dimension, which I have glimpsed and believe to be a most perfect state of existence, anything less than God consciousness would prohibit one from existing in this long sought after "Heaven on Earth". They seem to go hand in hand.

I have stressed in the Chapter *Observing the Paradoxes* to maximize your 3D experience by being all that you can be from moment to moment, while at the same time staying detached from the results. Considering this, coming into a state of God consciousness should greatly enhance your 3D experience, rather than cascading it into an untenable situation. In fact, if you believe yourself to have attained levels of God consciousness and are experiencing dark realities and reactions to your efforts, then you might consider that you may have deluded yourself into believing something that is not true by definition.

Remember that your Oversoul has its own agenda. High on its list of priorities is manifesting through you in a state of God consciousness, and that of achieving the 13D.

This concludes our series on the various types of Consciousness. It was in no way meant to be exhaustive, but rather as a reference and guideline for the lay person interested in pursuing expanded states of consciousness.

CHAPTER 55

FOCUSING ON THE LOWER THREE DIMENSIONS: LOWER DIMENSIONAL FOCUS

Here are some steps you can take to learn how to focus into the lower three dimensions, also known as the 3D.

This will help you avoid much of the agitation and fear associated with the approaching change of vibrations, occurring over the next several years.

As concerns you the personality, how can you help your Inner most Being, manifest through you, here in the 3D? After all, we are instructed to achieve serenity in the void of the 6D while we await our Oversoul. While this is a passive venture once achieved, I assure you that what follows for you is not.

Perhaps it will encourage you to know that your job is a relatively active one once you begin awakening, primarily because your Oversoul—working through your Soul—will be doing most of the important tasks while at the same time increasing its presence through you. In this and the Chapters that follow, I will detail exactly how to best work with your Soul, as concerns developing a three dimensional focus.

First Dimensional Focus

Most people function in physical consciousness in one of three ways. The first way is called the First Dimensional focus. This type of focus is characterized by a very narrow viewpoint and understanding of the world around them. A surprising characteristic of the 1D viewpoint is that this type of person often works harmoniously with others. They seem to make good workers because they are focused on making a living, and are not into conflict.

You may know some people like this. They may be very intelligent, but are contented with whatever life has dealt them. You will find 1D types in every walk of life. There are more 1D people on earth, than 2D and 3D peoples combined, numbering in the billions. Most 1D people are manual laborers, content with tending to everyday life and eking out a living for themselves and their families. One usually finds this type of person in third world countries, however you will also find them in all areas of life. They seem to know their place in society and are not concerned with politics, mainly because they feel powerless when it comes to larger issues.

This feeling of powerlessness may also explain the absolute devotion of the 1D type to various religions, which makes them easy targets for the more unscrupulous 2D types. Illiteracy is very wide spread in the 1D group. It may be interesting to note that it is the 1D people who riot under too much oppression from 2D types. The main spiritual lesson for the 1D person, is to become a 2D person.

Second Dimensional Focus

The second dimensional focus is attracted to conflict of various kinds. Conflicts that, interestingly enough, 2D people never attribute to conflict, but rather proudly wear it as a sort of righteous badge that says their side is right and the other side is wrong. Dichotomy, that so characterizes the 2D type of person, is the thread found running through every aspect of their lives. It is the 2D people, because of their ignorance of universal law, that have caused (and are causing) most of the problems that plague us today.

The Second Dimensional focus is easily spotted. For example, if a religion has as its foundation a dichotomy between "good and evil", then it is a 2D philosophy that fits nicely with 2D people. We find this same 2D conflict in everything from government to movie critics. 2D conflict goes unnoticed because it is considered normal by the 2D people who run everything and say what is normal and what is not.

2D people are always in the right. Many times they title themselves as right wing or the righteous verses the left (or wrong side). 2D people are busy defending themselves from their weaker discarded opposition, by building ever larger prisons. Even the mention of some sort of problem with their actions, and they will vigorously deny it, at the very least, and imprison or kill you in the more zealous countries. 2D people use 1D people. They will also use 2D people if they can get away with it. The main spiritual lesson for the 2D person, is to become a 3D person.

Third Dimensional Focus

Surprisingly, 3D people resemble 1D people. 3D people are no longer interested in conflict or taking sides on any issues. This is not because of a feeling of powerlessness, as is found in the 1D person. It is because of an intimate knowledge of universal law. The three dimensional focus is so perfectly balanced that it has no opposition.

There are very few 3D people on the planet today. Those who are here wield great power if they choose to use it. The third dimensional focus is primarily one of *manifestation*. A common prayer among 3D people is, "I pray only for God's will for me and the power to carry it out.".

Whem reading this, many 2D people will either claim that they indeed are 3D people or they will dismiss the whole thing as nonsense. The main spiritual lesson for the 3D person, is to successfully manifest their "Inner Being" by becoming one with it. To both allow and encourage more and more light to shine through, from the inside to the outside.

This Chapter and those that follow will be devoted to achieving 3D Consciousness and understanding the immediate importance for doing so as quickly as possible.

CHAPTER 56

FOCUSING ON THE LOWER THREE DIMENSIONS: THIRD DIMENSIONAL FOCUS (CONT.)

You may be wondering what all of the fuss is about? What does it matter if your focus is one, two, or three dimensional? After all, I am Gods creation in progress, and this is something that cannot be rushed. Like Popeye says, "I yams what I yams, and I canst be no more".

You certainly have a valid point, and normally I couldn't argue with you, however, there seems to be something wrong with our time-line. I am not the only one sensing this. Mystics from all over agree that they cannot see past the year 2012 which marks the end of the Mayan calender. Regardless of what these next seven years have in store for us, I will only comment on what I believe to be correct for this period of time and beyond.

Great changes occur at the dawning of any new Age. The reason for this is simple. In linear time, we are changing from one set of vibrations to another. In particular, we are changing from the reddish brown range of vibrations to the orange range of vibrations.

We, as humanity, have not experienced a change from one age to another since two thousand years ago. In terms of where we are, in the six thousand year long period called the "Dark Ages", we are moving out of the central portion of the dark ages and into the third and final two thousand year portion. Two thousand years from now, we will have a similar task as we move completely out of the dark Physical Ages, and into the Mental Ages.

According to history books, two thousand years ago there was a great spiritual upheaval with the advent of the World Teacher) who acted out, in his own life, the lessons for the two thousand year period just ending.

The birth of this Avatar was so significant to the people of that time that it marked the beginning of time, as pertains to how we number the years (B.C. and A.D.). Imagine how significant an event of this magnitude would be if it happened now. The point I am trying to make here is that the change from one Age to another is no small matter.

According to Time Traveler tenets, the final two thousand year period of any six thousand year period is Avatar-less. This means that there will be no central figure for the next two thousand years. The reason for this being that the final two thousand year period is a finalization of the previous four thousand years, in terms of planetary lessons to be learned.

As eventful as the beginning of the last two thousand year long Age was, it was nothing compared to the changes occurring now, and especially over the next several years. The reason for this is not very hard to understand. The change in vibration—two thousand years ago—was moving from brown vibrations to the reddish brown/burgundy part of the spectrum.

In contrast, the current transition entails moving from the reddish brown part of the spectrum, to orange. The result for the unprepared will be devastating.

The Tribulations

The Tribulations, or time of troubles, are a period of suffering, upheaval, sorrow, war and natural disaster.

Dispensationalism

Dispensationalism refers to the belief in a divine dispensation or ordering of events by God in a predetermined manner unaffected by and independent of human agency.

While these belief systems sound rather biblical, there is an element of truth contained within them. Advanced spiritual understanding can explain that what is transpiring are naturally occurring events that happen about every 26 thousand years, right around this time.

The intent of this Chapter and those that follow is to instill within you an understanding of the natural and logical nature of these next few years. Once armed with the *why*, one needs only to put into motion the *how*.

The why and how will be easily understood by studying the next several Chapters, and putting them into practice. I will be showing you easy to understand steps you can take in order to not only come through the "End Times", but to do it relatively unscathed.

Secondly, and more importantly, is my belief that if a sufficient number of people learn to practice Three Dimensional behavior, to the extent that the time loop—thought to be contained here in this time period—can be bypassed. This would insure a continuation of

Humanity's physical immortality, so that when we reach this present Age next time, we will have a continuous 32 thousand year recorded history.

In the next Chapter, I will share with you—among other things—my belief that the Master World Teacher, Jesus, has already been here in the "Second Coming", and has recently left the physical world, precipitating the final seven year period known as *The Tribulations*.

Chapter 57

Focusing on the Lower Three Dimensions: Lower Dimensional Focus (Cont.)

Let's look at the third dimensional viewpoint for a moment. We learned in earlier Chapters that the 2D is exactly the same as the 3D, except for the addition of forward motion (action) as an extra dimension. To put this into perspective, people with only a 2D focus usually cannot take action by themselves. They must be guided by outside forces that are managed by a few 3D people at the "top" of the food chain. This outside force is sometimes subtle, giving the 2D types the illusion of having 3D power. In business for example, a few 3D people delegate their 3D power and authority down through a pyramid structure. This structure is also found in most governments and religions.

2D people are perpetually embroiled in two-sided power struggles. Either on one side or the other. For them, there is only good versus evil, them or us, hot or cold, with very little shades of gray. 3D people on the other hand are balanced in the way a three legged stool is balanced compared to the two legged stool of a 2D person.

2D people are always out of balance whether they are aware of it or not. 3D people are always in balance and are always aware of it because they had to learn how to become 3D through balance and neutrality.

3D people found in high office can exhibit rhinoceros thick skin when dealing with the rant of hordes of 2D people who, of course, are lead by a 3D person.

Some 3D types become recluses, not wanting to exploit their 3D power. Charismatic religious leaders are always 3D people. Great sales persons, great personalities in music and film are often 3D people. And if the artist is not 3D at first, it is because a 3D person behind the scenes, is coaching and guiding them to become 3D.

I know of advanced 3D people who are spiritually aware enough not to get entangled with the not so aware 3D types. I have noticed that these spiritually aware 3D people use their 3D neutrality as a buffer between their internal serenity and physical turmoil just outside of their doors. Many move to more serene surroundings once they are financially secure enough to do so.

You will find mature 3D focused persons in business for themselves. They usually do not make good business heads because of their innate generosity. While lesser 3D focused people concentrate on making profit, the more spiritually educated 3D focused people concentrate on the welfare of their workers and clients, putting profit last. Understanding spiritual law as they do, they know that abundance is a natural state and that they will always have enough profit to be worthwhile.

Some 3D Guidelines

So, how can you become more 3D and less 2D? How does a spiritually knowledgeable 3D person conduct his/her affairs, walking through the same turmoil as you do, on a daily basis?

For starters, 3D people seem happier than 2D people. Let's look at this, for a moment, and see if we can spot the difference.

Being 3D means that a focus from deep within, is seeking to focus out through all of the dimensions, and like a microscope, focused into the third dimension. Being in touch with ones most inner self, naturally produces happiness, joy and freedom. But, in addition to this, there is the conscious act of being neutral.

There is an old occult maxim that says, "Be neither for or against". I take this to mean not to get involved in unimportant issues. If you notice, most people are heatedly passionate about something as benign as a football game. I know, I used to be one of these. This kind of misspent passion is a form of anti boredom. God forbid if a 2D person is in the least bored, even for a few minutes. Thus we have chronic TV watchers, book readers, and a host of other "simple pleasures". Don't get me wrong, I sometimes watch TV, love to read, and even go to a movie. The difference is that I like to do it, not have to do it. "All things in moderation".

Why is it desirable to become 3D, especially if you are happy being 2D? With the change in vibration we will be going through in the next several years, in addition to strange climatic conditions, and emotional instabilities that accompany these changes, many 2D types will not be able to cope emotionally. If you are currently 2D, you will, no doubt, be drawn into the 2D mass karma, as new balance points come into view. Those who cannot change for some reason, will not survive. The need for change will get more demanding as we come more into the new age.